THE ULTIMATE SURVIVAL APOTHECARY BIBLE

Unlock 500+ Ancient Remedies and Herbal Formulas to Heal, Thrive, and Stay Prepared for Any Emergency

Grace Hearthstone

Table Of Contents

Chapter 1: Introduction to the Survival Apothecary

1.1: Why an Apothecary Bible for Survival?

In today's world, where the unexpected can become reality in an instant, the value of being prepared cannot be overstated. The concept of a survival apothecary taps into the ancient wisdom of herbal remedies, connecting us to a time when self-sufficiency was not just an asset but a necessity for survival. This section delves into the critical importance of establishing your own herbal pantry, not just as a hobby but as a vital component of emergency preparedness.

Herbal remedies offer a dual advantage in survival scenarios: they provide us with the means to address health issues naturally and empower us with the knowledge to utilize the resources that surround us. Imagine facing a situation where access to conventional medicine is cut off due to natural disasters, economic downturns, or even more personal emergencies like sudden unemployment. In these moments, the ability to turn to a well-stocked herbal apothecary can make a significant difference in your well-being and that of your loved ones.

Building resilience through knowledge and preparation is at the heart of the survival apothecary. By learning to identify, harvest, and utilize medicinal plants, you not only equip yourself with the tools to treat ailments but also instill a sense of confidence and independence that comes from knowing you can care for your health under any circumstances. This resilience is crucial, not just for the individual but also for communities that might need to rely on shared resources in times of scarcity.

Practical applications of a survival apothecary are vast and varied. For example, knowing how to create a simple tincture from echinacea can help ward off colds and flu, while a salve made from comfrey and calendula can treat cuts and burns, reducing the risk of infection when medical help is not readily available. These skills, once common knowledge, have been overshadowed by the convenience of modern medicine but are no less valuable today, especially as we face an uncertain future.

Sustainability and self-sufficiency are additional benefits of embracing the survival apothecary philosophy. By growing your own herbs or ethically wildcrafting them, you reduce your reliance on pharmaceuticals and the commercial healthcare system, which can be both costly and environmentally damaging. This approach not only benefits your health and wallet but also contributes to a larger movement towards ecological stewardship and conservation.

Empowerment through education is a fundamental principle of the survival apothecary. By making this knowledge accessible to everyone, regardless of their background or experience with herbalism, we foster a community of informed individuals who can support and teach each other. This book aims to demystify the process of creating and using herbal remedies, providing clear, step-by-step instructions that anyone can follow, regardless of their prior knowledge or experience.

In conclusion, the survival apothecary is more than just a collection of remedies; it's a testament to the resilience and ingenuity of the human spirit. It represents a bridge between the past and the present, offering us a way to reconnect with the natural world and its healing powers. By incorporating these ancient practices into our modern lives, we prepare ourselves not only for the emergencies we hope never to face but also for a life of wellness, independence, and connection to the earth.

1.2: Rediscovering Ancient Wisdom for Modern Times

Integrating ancient herbal traditions into modern life involves a seamless blend of historical practices with contemporary needs, ensuring that the wisdom of the past serves the wellness of the present. The resurgence of interest in herbal remedies is not just a trend but a return to roots that have sustained human health for millennia. This section outlines practical ways to weave the power of herbs into the fabric of daily life, ensuring that ancient wisdom enriches modern living.

Herbal Gardens: Start by dedicating a small section of your home garden to herbs. Choose plants like **lavender**, **rosemary**, and **mint** for their versatility and ease of growth. These herbs require full sunlight for at least six hours a day, well-draining soil, and regular watering. For those with limited space, container gardening is a viable option. Use pots with drainage holes and place them on a south-facing windowsill to ensure they receive ample light.

Kitchen Pharmacy: Create a kitchen pharmacy where dried herbs, tinctures, and oils are within easy reach. Begin with commonly used herbs such as **turmeric** for inflammation, **ginger** for digestive issues, and **chamomile** for relaxation. Store dried herbs in airtight containers away from direct sunlight to preserve their potency. For tinctures, use a clear alcohol like vodka to extract the active compounds, and store the concoction in amber bottles to protect from light degradation.

Daily Rituals: Incorporate herbal remedies into daily rituals for a holistic approach to wellness. Start the day with a cup of **green tea** for its antioxidant properties. Introduce **adaptogenic herbs** like **ashwagandha** in your morning smoothie to help the body manage stress. For skincare, use **aloe vera** as a moisturizing agent and **tea tree oil** for its antimicrobial benefits. These practices not only provide physical benefits but also create moments of mindfulness and connection to nature.

Seasonal Living: Align herbal practices with the seasons for optimal health. In spring, focus on detoxifying herbs like **dandelion** and **nettle** to rejuvenate the body after winter. Summer calls for cooling herbs such as **peppermint** and **lemon balm** to soothe sun-exposed skin. In autumn, build immunity with **elderberry** and **echinacea**. Winter is the time for warming herbs like **cinnamon** and **ginger** to fend off colds and flu.

Community Engagement: Share the journey of rediscovering ancient wisdom with your community. Host herbal workshops, swap seeds and cuttings, and create a local herb exchange program. Engaging with others not only spreads knowledge but also fosters a sense of belonging and collective resilience.

Educational Resources: Continuously educate yourself on the history, cultivation, and use of herbs. Consult reputable sources, including herbal encyclopedias, scientific studies, and workshops offered by experienced herbalists. Knowledge is the foundation upon which safe and effective herbal practice is built.

By integrating these practices into modern life, we honor the legacy of our ancestors while adapting their wisdom to our contemporary needs. The revival of herbal traditions is a testament to their timeless relevance, offering natural, sustainable ways to enhance well-being. Through this integration, we not only nurture our health but also deepen our connection to the earth and its abundant healing gifts.

Chapter 2: Essential Tools and Ingredients

2.1: Setting Up Your Apothecary

To set up your home apothecary effectively, you'll need to focus on several key areas: selecting the right location, acquiring essential tools, sourcing quality ingredients, and organizing your space for both efficiency and preservation of your herbal remedies. Here's a detailed breakdown of each step to ensure you create a functional and practical apothecary at home.

Selecting the Right Location: Your apothecary should be in a cool, dry place away from direct sunlight, heat sources, and moisture. An ideal location could be a dedicated cabinet in your kitchen, a closet, or a room that stays relatively cool year-round. Ensure the area is away from household chemicals or strong food odors that could contaminate your herbs.

Acquiring Essential Tools:

1. **Glass Jars and Bottles**: Opt for amber or blue-colored glass to protect contents from UV light. You'll need a variety of sizes for storing dried herbs, tinctures, and oils.

2. **Digital Scale**: Precision is key in herbalism. A digital scale that measures in grams and ounces will ensure accurate dosing for your remedies.

3. **Mortar and Pestle or Electric Grinder**: Needed for grinding herbs and seeds. A mortar and pestle offer a more traditional approach, while an electric grinder provides efficiency.

4. **Fine Mesh Strainers and Cheesecloth**: For filtering tinctures, infusions, and decoctions. A selection of strainers in various sizes and a supply of cheesecloth are indispensable.

5. **Label Maker or Permanent Markers**: Proper labeling is crucial. Include the name of the herb, date of processing, and expiration date on each container.

6. **Measuring Spoons and Cups**: For precise ingredient measurements. Stainless steel or glass is preferred over plastic.

Sourcing Quality Ingredients: Start with a few basic herbs that are versatile and commonly used in herbal remedies. Lavender, chamomile, peppermint, and calendula are great starting points. Source your herbs from reputable suppliers or consider growing your own to ensure the highest quality and potency.

Organizing Your Space:

- **Herbs and Powders**: Store dried herbs and powders in clearly labeled jars. Organize alphabetically or by category (e.g., culinary, medicinal, teas) for easy access.

- **Tinctures and Oils**: Keep these in a separate area from dried herbs to prevent spills. Organize by type or purpose.

- **Tools and Supplies**: Designate a drawer or shelf for your tools and supplies, keeping them together so they are easy to find when you need them.

- **Work Area**: Maintain a clean, clutter-free work area with ample space for preparing your herbal remedies. This could be a section of your kitchen counter or a dedicated table in your apothecary space.

Remember, the key to a successful home apothecary is organization, quality, and precision. By carefully selecting your location, equipping yourself with the right tools, sourcing the best ingredients, and organizing your space effectively, you'll create a functional and efficient apothecary that serves your needs for natural healing and wellness.

2.2: Sourcing, Growing, and Storing Herbs

When sourcing herbs, the primary goal is to ensure they are of the highest quality, as this directly impacts their efficacy in your remedies. Begin by researching local herb farms or health food stores that prioritize organic and sustainable practices. When possible, opt for herbs certified organic by the USDA, as this guarantees they have been grown without synthetic pesticides or fertilizers. For those herbs not readily available locally, turn to reputable online suppliers who provide detailed information about their sourcing and processing methods. Always check reviews and possibly request batch-specific testing results for purity and contaminants.

Growing your own herbs is both rewarding and practical, allowing for the freshest ingredients at your fingertips. Start with easy-to-grow varieties such as **mint**, **basil**, and **lavender**. Choose a location that receives at least six hours of direct sunlight daily. Use high-quality, organic potting soil to ensure your herbs have the nutrients they need to thrive. For container gardening, ensure pots have adequate drainage holes to prevent root rot. Water your herbs in the early morning or late afternoon to minimize evaporation and apply a layer of mulch around the plants to retain soil moisture and suppress weeds. Implement companion planting to naturally deter pests and promote healthy growth; for example, planting basil near tomatoes can enhance flavor and repel insects.

Storing herbs properly is crucial to preserving their medicinal properties. Dried herbs should be kept in airtight containers made of dark glass or non-reactive metal, away from direct sunlight, heat, and moisture. Label each container with the herb's name, date of harvest, and expected shelf life to keep track of freshness. Most dried herbs will retain their potency for up to one year if stored correctly. For oils, tinctures, and salves, use amber or blue glass containers to protect against light degradation, and store in a cool, dark place. Regularly check your stored herbs for any signs of spoilage, such as mold or unusual odors, and discard any that do not meet quality standards.

By adhering to these guidelines for sourcing, growing, and storing herbs, you ensure that your survival apothecary is stocked with the best possible ingredients. This not only maximizes the effectiveness of your remedies but also supports a sustainable practice that benefits both your health and the environment.

Chapter 3: Safety Guidelines

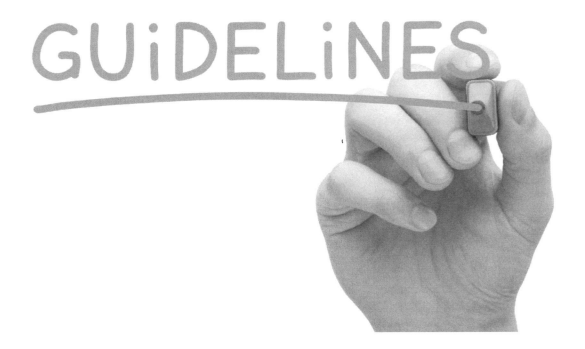

3.1: Understanding Dosages

When calculating **safe dosages** for herbal remedies, it's crucial to consider several factors including the individual's age, weight, health condition, and the potency of the herb. The process can seem daunting at first, but with a basic understanding and some practical examples, you can learn to navigate this essential aspect of herbal medicine safely.

Age is a significant determinant in dosage calculations. Generally, adults can handle more potent doses compared to children. For instance, if an adult dosage of Echinacea tincture is 1 teaspoon (about 5 ml), for a child aged 6-12, the dose should be reduced to 1/3 to 1/2 of the adult dose, depending on the child's size and health. For children under 6, consult a healthcare professional with expertise in herbal medicine.

Weight also plays a critical role. Many herbalists use the formula of 1 drop of herbal tincture per 1 kg of body weight as a starting point for determining the correct dose for an individual. This means a person weighing 70 kg might start with a dose of 70 drops of tincture, which can be adjusted based on the herb's effects and the individual's response.

When considering the **health condition** of the individual, it's important to start with lower doses for those with sensitivities or compromised health and gradually increase to the desired effect. This cautious approach helps prevent adverse reactions and allows for monitoring the herb's impact.

The **potency of the herb** is another critical factor. Herbs vary greatly in their strength and effects. For example, valerian root, known for its sedative properties, requires careful dosage adjustment as its potency can vary significantly between batches and brands. Starting with a lower dose and adjusting based on the desired effect is advisable.

Practical Example: Calculating Dosage for a Tincture

Let's calculate a safe starting dose for a valerian root tincture for an adult weighing 150 pounds (approximately 68 kg) using the 1 drop per kg body weight guideline:

1. **Calculate the individual's weight in kilograms**: 150 lbs / 2.2 = 68 kg
2. **Determine the starting dose based on weight**: 68 kg = 68 drops of tincture
3. **Adjust based on potency and individual response**: If the tincture is particularly potent or the individual is sensitive, start with half the calculated dose (34 drops) and adjust as needed.

Dosage Tables for Common Herbs

To simplify the process, here are indicative dosage tables for three common herbs:

1. **Echinacea (Immune Support)**

   - Adult: 1-2 teaspoons (5-10 ml) of tincture 3 times a day

   - Child (6-12 years): 1/3 to 1/2 of the adult dose

2. **Ginger (Digestive Aid)**

   - Adult: 2-4 grams of fresh root daily or 1 teaspoon (5 ml) of tincture

   - Child (6-12 years): 1/4 to 1/3 of the adult dose

3. **Chamomile (Sleep and Anxiety)**

   - Adult: 1-2 teaspoons (5-10 ml) of tincture before bed or 1-2 grams of dried herb in tea

   - Child (6-12 years): 1/3 to 1/2 of the adult dose in tea form

Conclusion

Understanding dosages is a foundational skill in herbal medicine, ensuring safety and efficacy in practice. By considering factors such as age, weight, health condition, and herb potency, and starting with conservative doses, you can confidently navigate the use of herbal remedies. Remember, when in doubt, consult with a professional, especially when administering herbs to children or individuals with health conditions.

3.2: Contraindications and Safe Practices

When incorporating herbal remedies into your wellness routine, it's crucial to be aware of **contraindications** and **safe practices**. This ensures that the natural solutions you turn to not only provide their intended benefits but also do so without causing harm. Here, we delve into common precautions and the interactions between herbs and pharmaceuticals, emphasizing the importance of safety in natural healing.

Contraindications refer to specific situations where an herb should not be used because it may cause adverse effects. These can vary widely depending on the individual's health conditions, medications they are currently taking, and even their pregnancy status. For example, while **St. John's Wort** is popular for its mood-enhancing properties, it can interact negatively with a wide range of medications, including birth control pills, leading to decreased effectiveness. Similarly, **Licorice Root**, known for its soothing effect on the digestive system, can elevate blood pressure when consumed in large quantities or over a long period, making it unsuitable for those with hypertension.

Understanding the potential for **herb-drug interactions** is equally important. Herbs can affect how drugs are metabolized in the body, either enhancing their effects, which may lead to toxicity, or inhibiting them, which can reduce their efficacy. For instance, **Grapefruit Juice** can increase the blood levels of certain medications, including statins and some blood pressure drugs, potentially leading to serious side effects. On the other hand, **Ginkgo Biloba**, often used for memory enhancement, can increase the risk of bleeding when taken with blood thinners like warfarin.

To navigate these concerns safely, consider the following steps:

1. **Consult Healthcare Professionals**: Before adding any new herb to your regimen, especially if you are taking prescription medications, consult with a healthcare provider knowledgeable in both conventional and herbal medicine.

2. **Start with Low Doses**: Begin with the lowest possible dose to see how your body reacts to the herb. This is particularly important if you are new to herbal remedies or have existing health conditions.

3. **Educate Yourself**: Invest time in learning about the herbs you are interested in. Understand not just their benefits but also their side effects, contraindications, and potential interactions with other substances.

4. **Monitor Your Body's Response**: Pay close attention to how your body responds to an herb. Look out for any adverse reactions, and if you experience any, discontinue use immediately and consult a healthcare professional.

5. **Keep Updated**: The field of herbal medicine is continuously evolving, with new research shedding light on herbs and their interactions. Stay informed about the latest findings to make educated decisions about your health.

6. **Maintain Accurate Records**: Keep a detailed record of all the herbs and medications you are taking, including dosages and frequency. This information can be invaluable for healthcare providers in managing your health effectively.

7. **Be Cautious with Pregnancy and Nursing**: Many herbs are not recommended during pregnancy or while breastfeeding due to the lack of sufficient research on their safety in these conditions. Always err on the side of caution and consult a healthcare professional.

By adhering to these guidelines, you can harness the power of herbal remedies safely and effectively, ensuring that your journey towards natural wellness is both beneficial and secure.

Chapter 4: The Herbalist's Mindset

4.1. Building Intuition for Natural Healing

To develop an intuition for natural healing, one must first cultivate a deep connection with the self and the natural world. This connection is not merely about recognizing the physical properties of herbs but understanding the subtle energies and the life force that they carry. Here are practical steps to build this intuition:

1. Spend Time in Nature: Begin by spending time in nature regularly. Whether it's a forest, a garden, or a park, immerse yourself in the natural world. Pay attention to the plants around you. Notice their colors, shapes, and how they grow. This practice helps to attune your senses to the natural world, fostering a deeper connection with plant life.

2. Learn to Meditate with Plants: Choose a plant or herb you feel drawn to and sit with it quietly. Meditate on its presence, focusing on its form, color, and aroma. Try to sense its unique energy. Meditation helps in developing a non-verbal communication with plants, allowing you to understand their healing properties beyond the physical level.

3. Practice Mindful Harvesting: When you're ready to collect herbs, whether from your garden or the wild, do so with mindfulness and respect. Before harvesting, take a moment to connect with the plant. You might even ask for permission in your own way. This practice helps to honor the life force of the plant and enhances the healing potential of the herbs you gather.

4. Create a Healing Space: Dedicate a space in your home where you can work with your herbs. It could be a small table or a corner in a room where you can blend your herbal preparations. Make this space sacred and inviting, a place where you feel calm and inspired. This environment will support your intuitive healing work.

5. Keep a Healing Journal: Document your experiences with different herbs and their effects on your body and spirit. Note any dreams, emotions, or insights that arise during your work with plants. Over time, this journal will become a valuable tool for understanding the subtle ways in which herbs communicate and assist in healing.

6. Trust Your Senses: As you work more with herbs, learn to trust your senses. Pay attention to the smells, tastes, and textures of herbs. Your body has an innate ability to recognize what it needs for healing. If you're drawn to a particular herb, explore its properties and consider how it might support your health.

7. Study Traditional Herbalism: While intuition is a powerful guide, grounding your practice in the knowledge of traditional herbalism can greatly enhance your understanding. Study the uses, benefits, and contraindications of herbs from reliable sources. This knowledge, combined with your intuition, will enable you to create effective and safe herbal remedies.

8. Connect with a Community: Joining a community of herbalists or natural healers can provide support and guidance as you develop your intuition. Sharing experiences and knowledge with others can inspire and deepen your practice.

9. Practice, Practice, Practice: Like any skill, building intuition takes time and practice. Work with herbs regularly, experiment with making your own remedies, and pay attention to the outcomes. With patience and dedication, your intuitive connection to the healing power of plants will grow.

By following these steps, you embark on a journey of discovery, connecting with the ancient wisdom of herbal medicine. This path is not just about learning to heal with plants but also about rediscovering your innate connection to the earth and its abundant healing gifts.

4.2. Connecting with Plants: The Spiritual Aspect

Fostering a spiritual connection with plants transcends the mere identification or use of them for healing purposes. It involves recognizing and engaging with the vibrant life force that plants embody. This connection can profoundly deepen your herbal practice, bringing a new dimension of understanding and respect for the natural world. To cultivate this spiritual bond, consider integrating the following exercises into your daily or weekly routines:

1. Plant Meditation: Choose a plant in your home, garden, or a natural area nearby. Sit or stand quietly in front of it, taking a few deep breaths to center yourself. Observe the plant without judgment, noticing its colors, textures, and how it interacts with its environment. Close your eyes and visualize the plant's energy field, imagining a luminous, vibrant light surrounding it. Try to connect with this energy, feeling a sense of oneness with the plant. This practice helps to develop a deeper, non-verbal communication with plants, enhancing your intuitive understanding of their healing properties.

2. Guided Visualization for Plant Connection: Begin by finding a comfortable, quiet space where you won't be disturbed. Close your eyes and visualize yourself walking in a lush, vibrant forest or garden filled with various plants and herbs. Imagine yourself being drawn to a specific plant or herb. As you approach it, reach out and gently touch it, feeling its unique energy pulsating. Ask the plant if it has a message or healing wisdom to share with you. Listen with your heart, remaining open to any sensations, emotions, or thoughts that arise. Thank the plant for its guidance and slowly bring your awareness back to your physical surroundings. This exercise can be particularly powerful for receiving insights about how specific plants can support your healing journey.

3. Herbal Offerings and Rituals: Creating small rituals or offerings can be a meaningful way to honor the plants you work with. This could be as simple as placing a bowl of water or a small crystal near your plants as a token of gratitude. You might also consider creating a small altar with items that represent the plant's elements (earth, air, fire, water) and spending time there meditating or setting intentions for your healing work. These acts of reverence acknowledge the reciprocal relationship between you and the plant kingdom, fostering a deeper spiritual connection.

4. Journaling with Plants: Keep a dedicated journal for your experiences and reflections on connecting with plants on a spiritual level. After spending time in meditation or visualization with a plant, write down any messages, feelings, or insights that came through. Note how your relationship with specific plants evolves over time and how they influence your physical, emotional, and spiritual well-being. This practice not only deepens your connection with plants but also serves as a valuable tool for personal growth and self-discovery.

5. Nature Walks with Intention: Regularly walking in nature with the intention of connecting spiritually with plants can open your awareness to the interconnectedness of all life. As you walk, silently or verbally express your gratitude for the plants and their healing gifts. Pay attention to any plants that seem to call out to you or capture your attention—this could be a sign that they have something to offer you on your healing journey.

6. Plant-based Dreamwork: Before going to bed, place a plant or herb you feel drawn to under your pillow or on your nightstand. Set an intention to receive healing messages or guidance from the plant in your dreams. Upon waking, take a moment to record any dreams or impressions you received in your journal. This practice can be a powerful way to tap into the subconscious mind and access deeper wisdom from the plant world.

By incorporating these exercises into your practice, you invite a profound sense of connection and reverence for the natural world into your life. This spiritual bond with plants not only enriches your herbal practice but also fosters a greater appreciation for the intricate web of life that sustains us all.

Book 2: History and Science of Herbal Healing

Chapter 5: The Legacy of Apothecary Medicine

5.1: From Ancient Civilizations to Modern Revival

The evolution of herbal practices from ancient civilizations to their modern revival is a testament to the enduring power of natural medicine. Across the globe, ancient cultures recognized the value of plants for healing, ritual, and daily well-being. This deep-rooted wisdom, passed down through generations, has experienced a resurgence in contemporary society as individuals seek sustainable, holistic approaches to health.

Ancient Egypt stands as one of the earliest civilizations to document medicinal plant use. Papyrus scrolls, such as the Ebers Papyrus, detail over 850 herbal prescriptions, highlighting the Egyptians' sophisticated understanding of herbal medicine. Ingredients like garlic, which was used for its broad-spectrum antimicrobial properties, and aloe vera, applied for its healing and soothing effects on wounds, are still widely used today.

Traditional Chinese Medicine (TCM), with its origins dating back over 5,000 years, embodies a holistic approach to health and healing. TCM utilizes an extensive pharmacopeia of herbs, such as ginseng for energy and vitality and licorice root for its harmonizing effects. The principles of TCM, including the balance of yin and yang and the flow of Qi, have gained international recognition, influencing modern herbal practices.

Ayurveda, the traditional system of medicine in India, incorporates a vast array of herbal remedies in its practice. Turmeric, with its anti-inflammatory and antioxidant properties, and ashwagandha, known for its adaptogenic qualities, are cornerstones of Ayurvedic medicine. These herbs are now celebrated in the West for their health benefits, illustrating the global exchange of herbal wisdom.

The Indigenous tribes of North America utilized the native flora for both medicinal and spiritual purposes. Echinacea, used by the Great Plains tribes for its immune-boosting properties, and white willow bark, valued for its pain-relieving salicin content, are examples of North American herbal practices influencing modern natural medicine.

The European tradition of herbalism, deeply influenced by the works of ancient Greek and Roman physicians such as Hippocrates and Galen, laid the groundwork for modern pharmacology. Lavender, used since ancient times for its calming and antiseptic properties, and chamomile, recognized for its soothing digestive and sedative effects, are staples in both traditional and contemporary herbalism.

The **modern revival** of herbal medicine can be attributed to a growing awareness of the limitations and side effects associated with synthetic drugs, alongside a desire to return to natural, sustainable health practices. This resurgence is supported by scientific research validating the efficacy of many traditional remedies, leading to an integration of herbal medicine into mainstream healthcare.

Educational institutions now offer programs in herbal medicine, reflecting its increasing acceptance. Furthermore, the internet has democratized access to herbal knowledge, enabling a DIY culture of health where individuals learn to cultivate, harvest, and prepare their own remedies.

Community gardens and urban foraging initiatives reconnect people with the natural world, fostering a sense of responsibility towards environmental stewardship and sustainability. This modern herbal movement, while rooted in ancient traditions, is distinctly forward-looking, emphasizing ecological balance, personal empowerment, and holistic well-being.

The transition from ancient wisdom to modern practice underscores a universal truth: the healing power of plants transcends time and culture. As we continue to explore the synergies between traditional knowledge and contemporary science, the future of herbal medicine holds immense potential for enhancing global health and sustainability.

5.2: How Herbal Remedies Shaped Human Survival

Throughout human history, herbal remedies have played a pivotal role in survival, transcending mere medicinal use to become integral components of daily life, emergency care, and preventive health strategies. This deep-rooted connection between humans and plants is evident in the way ancient civilizations utilized herbs for their multifaceted benefits, from treating acute ailments to enhancing overall well-being and longevity.

Ancient Civilizations and Herbal Medicine: Historical records from ancient Egypt, China, and Greece, among others, illustrate a sophisticated understanding of herbal medicine. The Ebers Papyrus, an Egyptian document dating back to 1550 BCE, lists over 850 herbal prescriptions, highlighting the use of garlic, juniper, cannabis, aloe, and mint for their healing properties. Similarly, Traditional Chinese Medicine (TCM) and Ayurveda, the ancient Indian system of medicine, have long incorporated a vast array of herbs like ginseng, turmeric, and ashwagandha, recognizing their potential to balance the body's energies and promote health.

Herbs in Emergency Situations: In times of crisis, the immediate availability and versatility of herbs have made them invaluable. Soldiers in ancient battles would carry basic herbal kits containing yarrow and comfrey for wound healing and pain relief. Similarly, sailors on long voyages relied on scurvy grass (rich in Vitamin C) to prevent scurvy, a life-threatening condition caused by Vitamin C deficiency. These practices underscore the role of herbs not only as curatives but as essential tools for survival in extreme conditions.

Preventive Health and Herbal Remedies: Beyond acute care, herbs have historically been used to strengthen the body's defenses against illness. The concept of "preventive health" is not new; it is deeply ingrained in the philosophy of herbal medicine. Adaptogens, a class of herbs including Rhodiola rosea and Eleuthero root, have been used for centuries to enhance resilience to stress and support overall vitality. This preventive approach is a testament to the ancient wisdom that views health as a holistic balance between the mind, body, and environment.

Cultural Significance and Transmission of Knowledge: The cultural importance of herbs is evident in the rituals, traditions, and folklore of various societies. This rich heritage of herbal knowledge was often passed down orally from one generation to the next, with healers, shamans, and wise women serving as the custodians of this precious wisdom. It is through this transmission of knowledge that the legacy of herbal remedies continues to influence modern survival strategies.

Modern Revival and Integration: Today, there is a resurgence of interest in herbal medicine as individuals seek natural, sustainable alternatives to pharmaceuticals. This modern revival is not merely a return to ancient practices but an integration of traditional wisdom with contemporary scientific research. The growing body of evidence supporting the efficacy of herbal remedies reinforces their value not only in treating and preventing disease but also in enhancing resilience, a critical aspect of survival in today's fast-paced world.

Chapter 6: Herbal Properties and Uses

6.1. Adaptogens, Antioxidants, and Antimicrobials

Adaptogens, antioxidants, and antimicrobials represent three pivotal categories of compounds found in herbs that have profound effects on human health. Understanding these properties and how to harness them through herbal remedies can empower individuals to maintain wellness, manage stress, and protect against illness.

Adaptogens are a unique class of healing plants that help balance, restore, and protect the body. They do not have a specific action but rather adapt their function according to the body's needs. An example of an adaptogen is **Ashwagandha (Withania somnifera)**, which has been shown to reduce cortisol levels, combat stress effects, and improve energy levels. To utilize Ashwagandha, consider incorporating it into a daily tonic. A general guideline is to use about 1 to 2 teaspoons of the powdered root in a cup of hot water or milk to make a nourishing drink. Start with the lower dosage to assess tolerance and gradually increase as needed.

Antioxidants play a crucial role in protecting the body from damage caused by free radicals, which are unstable molecules that can harm cellular structures. Herbs rich in antioxidants can support the immune system, reduce inflammation, and promote overall health. **Turmeric (Curcuma longa)**, known for its active compound curcumin, is a potent antioxidant. Incorporating turmeric into your diet can be as simple as adding a teaspoon of the ground spice to smoothies, soups, or teas. Combining turmeric with a pinch of black pepper can enhance the absorption of curcumin.

Antimicrobials offer defense against bacteria, viruses, and fungi, helping to prevent and fight infections. **Garlic (Allium sativum)** is a powerful antimicrobial herb that has been used for centuries. It contains allicin, a compound with broad-spectrum antimicrobial properties. To harness garlic's benefits, consider consuming 1-2 cloves of raw garlic daily, either minced in salad dressings or swallowed with water. For those sensitive to raw garlic, aged garlic supplements are a gentler alternative.

When incorporating these herbs into your regimen, it's important to source high-quality, organic herbs to ensure potency and purity. Also, understanding that each individual's response to herbs can vary is crucial; what works for one person may not work for another. Always start with lower doses to observe how your body reacts and consult with a healthcare professional, especially if you are pregnant, nursing, or on medication.

Adaptogens, antioxidants, and antimicrobials represent just the tip of the iceberg in the vast world of herbal medicine. By learning to utilize these powerful natural compounds, you can take significant steps toward enhancing your health and well-being, naturally and sustainably. Remember, the key to effective herbal remedy use is consistency and mindfulness about your body's responses.

6.2: The Science of Natural Healing

The science of natural healing delves into the intricate ways in which active compounds found in herbs interact with the human body, fostering health and combating illness. At the heart of this interaction is the body's innate ability to heal itself, a process that can be supported and enhanced through the strategic use of herbal remedies. Understanding the scientific principles behind this can empower individuals to make informed decisions about incorporating herbs into their health regimen.

Bioactive Compounds and Their Mechanisms: Plants produce a vast array of bioactive compounds, each with specific effects on the body. These include alkaloids, flavonoids, terpenes, and glycosides, among others. For instance, alkaloids, found in herbs like echinacea, can stimulate the immune system, while flavonoids, present in green tea, possess antioxidant properties that protect cells from oxidative stress and inflammation. Terpenes, which give lavender its distinctive aroma, can induce relaxation and improve sleep quality. Understanding these compounds and their mechanisms of action is crucial for harnessing the full potential of herbal remedies.

Synergy in Herbal Formulas: The concept of synergy is fundamental to the science of natural healing. When combined in the right proportions, certain herbs can enhance each other's effects, resulting in a more potent remedy than any single herb could achieve alone. This principle is evident in traditional formulations like the Chinese Four Thieves Vinegar, which combines multiple herbs to boost immunity and fight infection. Crafting effective herbal blends requires a deep understanding of each herb's properties and how they interact with one another.

Absorption and Metabolism: For herbal remedies to be effective, their active compounds must be absorbed into the bloodstream and reach the target tissues. Factors such as solubility, dosage form (e.g., tincture, tea, capsule), and the presence of other substances (e.g., piperine in black pepper enhancing curcumin absorption) can influence the bioavailability of these compounds. Once absorbed, these compounds are metabolized by the liver, where they can exert their therapeutic effects or be transformed into metabolites with their own activity.

Individual Responses to Herbal Remedies: It's important to recognize that individuals may respond differently to the same herbal remedy due to variations in genetics, health status, and concurrent use of medications. These differences can affect not only the efficacy of the remedy but also the risk of adverse effects. Personalizing herbal treatments involves considering these factors and adjusting dosages accordingly, often through trial and observation, to find the optimal regimen for each individual.

Safety and Efficacy: While many herbs have a long history of use and are generally considered safe, rigorous scientific studies are essential to validate their efficacy and safety. Clinical trials and pharmacological research contribute to our understanding of how herbs work, their potential health benefits, and any risks associated with their use. This research is vital for integrating herbal medicine into modern healthcare in a way that is both safe and evidence-based.

Integrating Science and Tradition: The science of natural healing is not just about isolating active compounds or conducting clinical trials; it's also about respecting and integrating the traditional knowledge that has guided herbal medicine for centuries. By combining empirical evidence with historical wisdom, practitioners of herbal medicine can develop more effective, holistic approaches to health and wellness.

Chapter 7: Herbs in Cultural and Historical Contexts

7.1. Sacred and Ritualistic Uses of Herbs

Throughout history, herbs have played a crucial role not only in the physical healing practices of various cultures but also in their spiritual and ritualistic traditions. These practices, deeply rooted in the belief systems of communities around the world, offer a fascinating glimpse into the sacred relationship between humans and the plant kingdom. By exploring these traditions, we can gain insight into the profound respect and reverence our ancestors had for the natural world, and perhaps rekindle a similar connection in our modern lives.

Native American Traditions: In many Native American cultures, sage, specifically white sage (Salvia apiana), is considered sacred and is used in smudging ceremonies to purify spaces, objects, and individuals. The smoke from burning sage is believed to cleanse negative energy, promote healing, and offer protection. Similarly, sweetgrass (Hierochloe odorata), known for its sweet, aromatic scent, is often burned in conjunction with sage to invite positive spirits and energies.

Ayurveda and Holy Basil: Ayurveda, the traditional system of medicine in India, incorporates a holistic approach to health, emphasizing the balance between body, mind, and spirit. Holy basil or Tulsi (Ocímum sanctum) is revered in Ayurveda and Hinduism as an embodiment of the goddess Tulsi, offering divine protection. Consumed as a tea or used in daily worship, holy basil is believed to purify the aura, enhance spiritual growth, and promote longevity.

Traditional Chinese Medicine and Ginseng: In Traditional Chinese Medicine (TCM), ginseng (Panax ginseng) is highly valued for its adaptogenic properties, believed to harmonize the various systems of the body. Beyond its medicinal use, ginseng is also associated with spiritual potency, often used in rituals to attract health, prosperity, and spiritual wisdom. The root's human-like form is thought to embody the essence of Earth and Heaven, bridging the gap between the physical and spiritual realms.

European Pagan and Wiccan Practices: In European pagan and Wiccan traditions, herbs are integral to rituals and spells, each plant possessing its own magical properties. Mugwort (Artemisia vulgaris), for example, is often used for protection during travel and to induce prophetic dreams. It is burned as incense during rituals to enhance psychic abilities and facilitate astral projection. Lavender, with its calming scent, is used in love spells and to promote peace and harmony.

African Traditional Medicine: In many African cultures, herbs are used not only for healing but also in ceremonies and rituals to communicate with ancestral spirits. The African dream herb (Entada rheedii), for instance, is used to induce vivid dreams that allow communication with the spirit world, providing guidance and insight. Rituals involving herbs often include offerings, chants, and dances, emphasizing the connection between the physical and spiritual health of the individual and the community.

Shamanic Practices in the Amazon: The Amazon rainforest, with its vast biodiversity, is home to a rich tradition of shamanic medicine. Ayahuasca, a brew made from the Banisteriopsis caapi vine and other plants, is used in ceremonial contexts for deep spiritual exploration, healing, and communion with the spirit world. Shamans, or medicine men and women, guide participants through the experience, which is believed to reveal the interconnectedness of all living things and offer profound insights into one's life and purpose.

These examples represent just a fraction of the myriad ways in which herbs are woven into the spiritual fabric of cultures worldwide. By understanding and respecting these traditions, we can appreciate the depth of our connection to the natural world and explore ways to incorporate these ancient wisdoms into our own practices for healing and spiritual growth.

7.2: Sacred and Ritualistic Uses of Herbs

In the realm of spiritual and ritualistic practices, herbs serve as powerful conduits for connecting the physical world with the metaphysical, embodying the essence of life's energy and the universe's profound mysteries. These sacred botanicals are not merely substances for physical healing but are deeply woven into the fabric of spiritual rituals across diverse cultures, each herb carrying its unique vibrational energy and purpose.

White Sage (Salvia apiana), for instance, is held in high esteem within Native American traditions for its purifying and protective properties. A bundle of dried white sage, when lit and smoldered, produces a fragrant smoke that is meticulously wafted around a person or space using a feather or hand. This act, known as smudging, is believed to clear negative energies, creating a clean slate for spiritual work and fostering an environment of peace and protection. The ritual underscores a profound respect for the plant's spirit, acknowledging its power to cleanse and guard the sacredness of life.

Palo Santo (Bursera graveolens), a sacred wood from South America, is similarly used in cleansing and healing ceremonies. Its sweet, resinous scent, released when the wood is burned, is thought to enter the energy field of ritual participants, clearing misfortune, negative thoughts, and evil spirits. The use of Palo Santo is deeply rooted in the spiritual traditions of the Indigenous peoples of the Andes. Before burning, it is customary to state one's intention or prayer, thus activating the wood's spiritual properties and aligning the ritual with the user's specific needs.

Frankincense (Boswellia sacra) and **Myrrh (Commiphora myrrha)**, resins derived from the sap of trees, have been used in spiritual practices for thousands of years, most notably within Christian, Judaic, and Islamic traditions. Burned as incense during religious ceremonies, these resins are believed to elevate prayers to the divine, purify the atmosphere, and facilitate a deeper state of spiritual awareness. The act of burning frankincense and myrrh is a ritual in itself, symbolizing the transformation of the physical to the spiritual, the resin's smoke carrying prayers from the earthly plane to the heavens.

Holy Basil (Tulsi, Ocimum sanctum), revered in Hinduism as a manifestation of the goddess Lakshmi, is cultivated in many Indian homes for its spiritual sanctity and medicinal value. Leaves of Tulsi are offered in daily worship as a symbol of devotion and purity, believed to open the heart and mind to the divine. Consuming Tulsi in tea or as a part of ritual offerings is thought to protect and bless the individual and their family, promoting health, happiness, and spiritual well-being.

Cedar (Cedrus), used in various forms by Indigenous peoples of North America, serves as a medicine for purification and protection. Cedar branches are often placed in homes or used in sweat lodge ceremonies to invite positive energies, cleanse the space, and provide grounding. The burning of cedar acts as a bridge between the physical and spiritual worlds, its smoke carrying prayers and intentions, while its presence in a home is a constant reminder of the sacredness of life and the natural world.

Incorporating these sacred herbs into one's spiritual practice requires mindfulness and respect for the plant's spirit and the cultural traditions from which these practices originate. Engaging with these herbs in a ritualistic context is not merely about the physical act but involves an open heart, clear intention, and a deep connection to the spiritual essence of the plant. Whether used for smudging, as incense, in prayer, or as an offering, these sacred botanicals offer a pathway to deepen one's spiritual practice, connect with the divine, and honor the interconnectedness of all life.

Book 3: Mastering Herbal Preparations

Chapter 8. Herbal Preparation Basics

When embarking on the journey of creating your own herbal preparations, understanding the basics of tinctures and infusions is essential. These methods are foundational for any apothecary, allowing for the extraction and preservation of the medicinal properties of herbs. To start, let's delve into the art of making tinctures, which involves soaking herbs in alcohol or vinegar to extract their active components. The choice between alcohol and vinegar as a solvent depends on the intended use of the tincture and personal preference, especially for those avoiding alcohol. For alcohol-based tinctures, a high-proof spirit, typically 80-proof vodka, is ideal due to its ability to dissolve a wide range of plant constituents and its preservation qualities. Vinegar, while not as potent as alcohol in extracting certain compounds, offers a non-alcoholic alternative that still effectively preserves the beneficial properties of herbs.

The process begins by filling a clean, dry jar about half to two-thirds full with dried herbs. Fresh herbs can also be used, but they should be finely chopped and the jar should be filled to accommodate their greater volume. Next, pour the alcohol or vinegar over the herbs until they are completely submerged, leaving about an inch of liquid above the herbs to allow for expansion. Seal the jar tightly and label it with the date and contents. The mixture should then be stored in a cool, dark place, shaking it daily to encourage extraction. After four to six weeks, the tincture should be strained through a fine mesh strainer or cheesecloth, squeezing out as much liquid as possible. The final step is to transfer the liquid to a clean, dark glass bottle for storage. Tinctures can last for several years when stored properly, away from light and heat.

Infusions, on the other hand, are akin to making tea and are an excellent way to extract the more delicate components of herbs, such as volatile oils and flavors. To prepare an herbal infusion, boiling water is poured over herbs and allowed to steep for a specific period, usually 15 to 20 minutes for leaves and flowers, and up to several hours for roots and barks to ensure the maximum extraction of beneficial properties. The choice of container for steeping is important; a teapot or jar that can be covered will help to retain heat and prevent the escape of volatile compounds. After steeping, the mixture is strained, and the resulting liquid can be consumed immediately or stored for a short period in the refrigerator.

Both tinctures and infusions offer versatile and effective means of harnessing the healing power of herbs. Whether used for their therapeutic benefits or simply to enjoy the flavors of nature, mastering these techniques is a fundamental step in building your survival apothecary. As we continue to explore herbal preparation basics, we'll delve into more advanced techniques and considerations to further enhance your apothecary skills.

Decoctions and salves represent another crucial aspect of herbal preparations, expanding the apothecary's toolkit for creating potent remedies. Decoctions are particularly suited for extracting the active constituents from tougher plant materials, such as roots, barks, and hard seeds. The process involves simmering the plant material in water for an extended period, typically ranging from 20 minutes to several hours, depending on the hardness of the material. This slow cooking method allows for the breakdown of cell walls and the release of soluble compounds into the water. To prepare a decoction, one should start with cold water and the plant material, gradually bringing the mixture to a boil and then reducing it to a simmer, ensuring that the pot is covered to prevent the loss of water and volatile substances. After simmering, the liquid is strained and can be taken directly or stored for a few days in the refrigerator.

Salves, on the other hand, are semi-solid preparations used topically to heal and protect the skin. They are made by infusing herbs in oils to extract their therapeutic properties, followed by combining the infused oil with beeswax to achieve the desired consistency. The choice of oil is important, with olive oil being a popular option due to its stability and skin-nourishing properties. To create an herbal salve, one must first gently heat the chosen oil and add dried herbs, allowing the mixture to infuse over low heat for several hours. Care must be taken to avoid overheating, which can degrade the herb's beneficial properties. After infusion, the oil is strained and then reheated with beeswax until the wax melts. The hot mixture is then poured into containers and allowed to cool, solidifying into a protective salve.

For both decoctions and salves, precision in measurement and attention to detail are paramount. The ratio of plant material to water or oil, the choice of container, and the duration of cooking or infusion are all factors that influence the effectiveness of the final product. Additionally, documenting the process and outcomes in a journal can provide valuable insights for future preparations, allowing for adjustments and improvements.

Understanding these basic yet diverse methods of herbal preparation equips the survival apothecary with a broad range of options for addressing various health concerns and conditions. From the soothing relief of a salve to the deep healing potential of a decoction, these techniques form the backbone of natural medicine. As one becomes more proficient in these methods, experimenting with different herbs and combinations can lead to the development of personalized remedies tailored to specific needs, further enhancing the resilience and self-sufficiency of the herbal practitioner.

8.1: Tinctures and Infusions Basics

When creating **tinctures**, the ratio of herb to solvent is crucial for achieving the desired potency. A common starting point is a 1:5 ratio, where one part of dried herb is combined with five parts of alcohol or vinegar. For fresh herbs, due to their higher water content, a 1:2 ratio is often used. Precision in measurement ensures consistency across batches, so using a kitchen scale to weigh the herbs and a measuring cup for the solvent is recommended. After combining the herb and solvent in the jar, it's essential to ensure that the herbs are fully submerged to prevent mold growth. A common practice is to use a piece of parchment paper under the lid to keep the herbs submerged while allowing the mixture to breathe.

For **infusions**, the type of herb and the desired strength dictate the amount of herb and water. A general guideline for a standard infusion is to use one teaspoon of dried herb or two teaspoons of fresh herb per cup of boiling water. However, for stronger medicinal teas, such as those intended for therapeutic use, the ratio can be increased to one tablespoon of dried herb per cup of water. Ensuring the water is freshly boiled and poured directly over the herbs maximizes the extraction of their medicinal properties. Covering the steeping vessel is a critical step that prevents the evaporation of volatile oils and maintains the infusion's therapeutic quality.

Decoctions require a longer extraction process, especially when working with hard, woody materials or roots. Starting with cold water, add the herbs, and slowly bring the mixture to a boil. Lowering the heat and simmering for an extended period allows for the extraction of soluble constituents. A standard ratio for decoctions is one part herb to eight parts water, simmered until the volume is reduced by half. This concentrates the decoction, making it a potent remedy. Using a covered stainless steel or glass pot prevents contamination and ensures that no beneficial compounds are lost during the simmering process.

When preparing **salves**, the infusion of herbs into oil is the first step. A ratio of one part dried herb to ten parts oil is a good starting point for creating a potent herbal oil. Slowly heating the oil and herbs together for several hours on low heat facilitates the transfer of medicinal properties to the oil. Straining the herbs using cheesecloth ensures a clear, herb-free oil, which can then be combined with beeswax. The amount of beeswax added determines the firmness of the salve; a ratio of one part beeswax to eight parts oil creates a firm, yet spreadable, salve. Pouring the mixture into tins or jars while still liquid and allowing it to cool undisturbed results in a smooth, professional-looking salve.

Each of these methods—tinctures, infusions, decoctions, and salves—serves a specific purpose in the herbal apothecary, offering various ways to harness the healing power of plants. By adhering to these guidelines and ratios, even beginners can create effective, natural remedies at home. As skills and confidence grow, experimenting with different herbs, combinations, and concentrations can lead to the development of unique, personalized herbal remedies tailored to specific needs and preferences.

8.2. Decoctions and Salves

To further our exploration into the realm of herbal preparations, let's delve into the specifics of creating **decoctions** and **salves**. These methods, while ancient, are incredibly effective for extracting and utilizing the potent medicinal properties of tougher plant materials and for creating topical applications to address a myriad of skin issues and injuries.

Decoctions are an ideal method for extracting the healing properties from the more resilient parts of plants, such as roots, barks, and dense herbs. The process begins by coarsely chopping or grinding the plant material to increase the surface area exposed to water. For every cup of water, use one tablespoon of dried herb or two tablespoons of fresh herb. Place the plant material in a pot and cover it with cold water. Slowly bring the mixture to a boil, then reduce the heat and simmer gently. Cover the pot to prevent the evaporation of water and volatile oils. The simmering time can vary depending on the plant material's density; roots and barks may require 20 to 40 minutes, while tougher seeds might need up to an hour. Once the volume of water has reduced by about one-third, remove the pot from heat and strain the decoction while it's still hot. Decoctions are best used immediately but can be stored in the refrigerator for up to 48 hours.

Salves, on the other hand, are semi-solid healing applications made by infusing oils with herbs and then thickening the mixture with beeswax. To start, choose a carrier oil—olive oil is a popular choice due to its stability and beneficial properties for the skin. Measure one cup of carrier oil and add about a quarter cup of dried herbs. Gently heat the oil and herbs in a double boiler, keeping the temperature low to avoid frying the herbs. Simmer for two to three hours to allow the herbs' medicinal properties to infuse into the oil. After infusion, strain the oil through cheesecloth to remove all plant material, squeezing out as much oil as possible. Return the infused oil to the double boiler and add beeswax; a general guideline is about one ounce of beeswax per cup of infused oil for a firm salve. Heat gently until the beeswax is completely melted. Test the consistency by placing a small amount on a spoon and cooling it in the refrigerator. If the salve is too soft, add more beeswax; if too hard, add more oil. Once the desired consistency is achieved, pour the mixture into clean tins or jars and let it cool and solidify.

For both decoctions and salves, labeling is crucial. Include the name of the remedy, the date it was made, and the expiration date. Decoctions are generally best used within a couple of days when stored in the refrigerator, while salves, kept in a cool, dark place, can last for up to a year. Always document the ratios of ingredients used and any observations about the preparation process or the effectiveness of the remedy. This practice will help refine your techniques and formulations over time.

By mastering the art of making decoctions and salves, you equip yourself with the knowledge to extract the full spectrum of medicinal properties from plants and create potent, natural remedies for a wide range of ailments. These preparations are not only a testament to the enduring wisdom of herbal medicine but also a powerful addition to your home apothecary, offering natural, effective solutions for health and wellness.

Chapter 9: Advanced Techniques

9.1: Extracting Potency with Alcohol, Vinegar, and Oil

Moving forward with the extraction of active principles using **alcohol, vinegar, and oil infusions**, it's crucial to understand the nuances that make each solvent unique and how to leverage them for the most effective herbal remedies. Each solvent has its own set of characteristics that can either enhance or diminish the medicinal properties of the herbs being used. Here, we'll dive into the specifics of each solvent and provide guidelines for their optimal use.

Alcohol is renowned for its ability to dissolve a wide range of plant constituents, making it the solvent of choice for creating potent tinctures. When selecting alcohol for tinctures, aim for a neutral spirit with a high alcohol content, typically around 40-50% alcohol by volume (ABV), such as vodka or brandy. This concentration is ideal for extracting both water-soluble and alcohol-soluble compounds. For herbs rich in resinous compounds or essential oils, a higher alcohol concentration, up to 95% ABV, may be necessary. The process involves macerating the herbs in alcohol for a period of 4 to 6 weeks, shaking the container daily to ensure thorough extraction. After this period, the mixture is strained, and the tincture is stored in amber glass bottles to protect it from light degradation.

Vinegar, especially apple cider vinegar, offers a compelling alternative for those seeking a non-alcoholic medium. Vinegar excels in extracting minerals and other water-soluble compounds from herbs. Its acidic nature also acts as a preservative, extending the shelf life of the infusion. To prepare an herbal vinegar, fill a jar with chopped or crushed herbs, then cover them completely with vinegar, ensuring there's at least a couple of inches of vinegar above the herb material. Seal the jar with a non-metallic lid or place a barrier between the jar and a metal lid to prevent corrosion. Let the mixture sit for 3 to 4 weeks, shaking it daily. Strain the vinegar into clean bottles, label, and store in a cool, dark place. Herbal vinegars can be used internally or as a base for salad dressings and marinades, offering a way to incorporate herbal remedies into daily meals.

Oil infusions are ideal for creating topical herbal remedies, capturing the lipophilic (fat-soluble) compounds present in many medicinal plants. Olive oil is a popular choice due to its stability and skin-nourishing properties, but almond, coconut, and jojoba oils are also excellent carriers. To make an oil infusion, fill a jar halfway with dried herbs and cover them with your chosen carrier oil, ensuring there's at least an inch of oil above the herbs to allow for expansion. Place the jar in a warm, sunny spot or in a water bath on low heat for a slow infusion, typically 2-4 weeks, or use a double boiler for a more rapid infusion, heating the mixture gently for a few hours. Once the infusion is complete, strain the oil through cheesecloth, squeezing out as much oil as possible, and transfer it to clean bottles or jars for storage. Infused oils can be used directly on the skin, incorporated into salves and balms, or used as massage oils.

Each solvent brings out different properties in the herbs, and understanding these characteristics allows for the creation of a wide array of herbal remedies tailored to specific needs. Whether you're crafting tinctures for internal use, vinegars for culinary applications, or oils for topical treatments, the key is to match the solvent to the herb's active constituents and the intended use of the final product. By mastering these techniques, you can expand your herbal apothecary and enhance your ability to address a variety of health concerns with natural, homemade remedies.

9.2: Herbal Powders and Capsules

Creating **herbal powders** involves drying herbs thoroughly before grinding them into a fine powder. This process preserves the herbs' medicinal properties and makes them easy to incorporate into capsules, teas, or food. To start, select fresh herbs, preferably harvested at their peak potency, which is often in the morning after the dew has evaporated but before the sun is too strong. Rinse the herbs gently to remove any dirt or insects, and pat them dry with a clean towel. For drying, you can use a dehydrator set at a low temperature (95-115°F) to preserve the herbs' active compounds. Spread the herbs in a single layer on the dehydrator trays, ensuring they are not overlapping too much, which could lead to uneven drying. The drying time will vary depending on the herb and the thickness of the leaves or flowers; it can take anywhere from 1 to 4 hours. Check the herbs periodically, and once they are brittle and crumble easily between your fingers, they are ready to be ground.

For grinding, a coffee grinder or a mortar and pestle can be used. If using a coffee grinder, pulse the dried herbs in short bursts to avoid overheating, which can lead to loss of potency. Sieve the ground herbs through a fine mesh to achieve a uniform powder, re-grinding any larger pieces that don't pass through. Store the herbal powder in airtight containers, labeled with the herb's name and the date of processing, in a cool, dark place to maintain their potency.

Capsulating herbal powders is a convenient way to take herbs, especially those with an unpleasant taste or for precise dosage control. Capsule machines are available and can be a worthwhile investment for those planning to make capsules regularly. These machines typically come with a base, a top, a tamper, and a spreader card. To fill capsules:

1. Separate the capsule shells into their two halves.

2. Place the longer half of the capsules into the base of the capsule machine.

3. Fill the capsules with your herbal powder using the spreader card to evenly distribute the powder over the holes. Use the tamper to pack the powder down firmly.

4. Once filled, place the shorter half of the capsule on top and use the machine's mechanism to press the two halves together.

5. Remove the filled capsules from the machine and store them in a labeled, airtight container.

When creating **herbal mixtures** for capsules, consider the desired outcome of the remedy. For example, a blend for aiding sleep may include herbs like valerian root, passionflower, and chamomile in equal parts. To calculate the dosage, research the recommended daily intake for each herb and adjust the ratios accordingly. It's crucial to start with small doses to see how your body reacts, as individual sensitivity to herbs can vary widely.

For those new to using herbal remedies, it's advisable to consult with a healthcare provider or a trained herbalist, especially if you are pregnant, nursing, or taking prescription medications, to avoid any potential adverse reactions or interactions. With careful preparation and attention to detail, creating your own herbal powders and capsules can be a rewarding way to enhance your wellness routine, offering a natural and personalized approach to health.

Chapter 10. The Art of Blending Herbs

10.1: Creating Herbal Formulas for Specific Needs

When developing herbal formulas for specific needs, it's crucial to understand the unique properties of each herb and how they can synergistically work together to enhance their effectiveness. The process involves a careful selection of herbs based on their medicinal properties, desired effects, and compatibility with each other. Here are detailed steps and considerations for creating targeted herbal blends:

1. **Identify the Primary Health Concern or Goal**: Begin by clearly defining the primary health issue or wellness goal you aim to address with your herbal formula. Whether it's boosting immunity, relieving stress, improving digestion, or supporting sleep, having a clear objective guides the selection of appropriate herbs.

2. **Research Herb Properties**: For each health concern, research herbs known for their efficacy in that area. Focus on herbs with a history of use for similar issues, documented in herbal compendiums or supported by contemporary research. Pay attention to their active constituents, therapeutic actions (e.g., anti-inflammatory, sedative, digestive), and any potential side effects or contraindications.

3. **Consider Herb Synergy**: Look for herbs that complement each other's actions. Synergy occurs when the combined effect of the herbs is greater than the sum of their individual effects. For example, combining ginger (Zingiber officinale) with turmeric (Curcuma longa) can enhance anti-inflammatory effects due to their complementary active compounds.

4. **Choose a Suitable Form**: Decide on the most appropriate form for your blend, such as a tea, tincture, capsule, or topical salve. The choice depends on the intended use, the specific herbs selected (some are more effective in certain forms), and user preference. For instance, digestive herbs might be best utilized in a tea for direct contact with the digestive system, while a salve might be preferred for a localized skin issue.

5. **Determine Proportions**: Establishing the right proportions of each herb in your blend is critical. Start with a simple formula, typically three to five herbs, to ensure each can contribute effectively without being diluted by too many components. Use a dominant herb that addresses the primary concern, supported by secondary herbs that enhance the primary action or offer complementary benefits. Adjust ratios based on the potency of the herbs and the desired strength of the formula.

6. **Test and Adjust**: Create a small batch of your herbal blend and monitor its effectiveness. It may take several iterations to find the right combination and proportions. Be prepared to adjust the formula based on feedback or observed results. Documentation during this phase is crucial for refining the blend and replicating success in future batches.

7. **Safety and Dosage**: Always prioritize safety by adhering to recommended dosages, especially when working with potent herbs. Consult reliable herbal references or a professional herbalist to confirm safe usage amounts and to ensure that your blend does not interact negatively with any medications or conditions.

8. **Labeling and Record-Keeping**: Properly label your herbal formula with ingredients, proportions, date of creation, and intended use. Keep detailed records of your research, formulation process, and any adjustments made over time. This documentation is invaluable for replicating successful blends and tracking the efficacy of different formulas.

By following these detailed steps, you can create effective, safe, and personalized herbal formulas tailored to specific health needs. This approach not only harnesses the therapeutic power of individual herbs but also leverages the enhanced benefits of their synergy, offering a holistic solution to health and wellness concerns.

10.2: Balancing Flavors and Effects

Balancing the flavors and effects of herbs in your remedies is as much an art as it is a science. The goal is to create a concoction that not only serves its therapeutic purpose but is also enjoyable to consume. This can be particularly challenging given the potent and sometimes bitter tastes of many medicinal herbs. Here are strategies to achieve a harmonious balance:

Understand the Flavor Profile of Each Herb: Every herb comes with its unique flavor profile—bitter, sweet, sour, pungent, or astringent. Recognizing these flavors is the first step in creating a balanced remedy. For instance, the bitterness of dandelion root can be offset with the sweetness of licorice root or the tanginess of orange peel.

Incorporate Natural Sweeteners: Sweeteners can greatly enhance the palatability of herbal remedies. Consider adding honey, agave syrup, or stevia not just for their sweetening effects but also for their health benefits. Honey, for example, is known for its antibacterial properties and can add a soothing texture to teas and syrups.

Use Complementary Flavors: Just as in cooking, combining herbs with complementary flavors can create a more complex and pleasant taste. A classic example is peppermint and chamomile, where the coolness of peppermint balances the mild sweetness of chamomile, making for a relaxing tea blend.

Adjusting Textures: The texture of a remedy can affect its overall sensory experience. For thicker preparations like salves or syrups, consider the mouthfeel. Oils like coconut or almond can smooth out salves, while glycerin can add a silky texture to syrups without affecting blood sugar levels.

Experiment with Acidic Components: A hint of acidity can brighten the flavors in a remedy and add a refreshing note. Lemon juice, apple cider vinegar, or tamarind paste can be used sparingly to lift the overall profile of the remedy and add a layer of complexity to the taste.

Consider the Therapeutic Impact of Flavors: Beyond taste, the flavors themselves can contribute to the healing properties of the remedy. Bitter herbs stimulate digestion, while sour flavors can have a cooling effect. Sweet flavors often soothe and calm. Thus, balancing flavors also means balancing the therapeutic effects.

Layering Flavors: Start with a base flavor and build upon it with complementary and contrasting notes. For instance, a base of green tea can be layered with the floral notes of lavender and the sharpness of ginger to create a tea that is both invigorating and soothing.

Trial and Error: Developing the perfect blend often requires experimentation. Start with small batches and adjust the proportions of each ingredient until you achieve the desired balance of flavors and effects. Keep detailed notes of each variation so you can replicate or adjust the formula in future batches.

Solicit Feedback: Sometimes, our own taste preferences can bias our creations. Getting feedback from others can provide new insights and suggestions for improving the balance of flavors in your remedies.

Herbal Pairings and Ratios: Certain herbs naturally complement each other, not just in flavor but in therapeutic action. For example, turmeric is often paired with black pepper to enhance its bioavailability. The ratio of these pairings is crucial; too much black pepper can overwhelm the subtle warmth of turmeric.

By applying these strategies, you can transform your herbal remedies from merely medicinal to pleasantly palatable, ensuring that they are not only effective but also enjoyable to use. This approach not only enhances the user experience but also encourages consistent use of the remedy, maximizing its health benefits.

Chapter 11: Fermented Herbal Preparations

11.1: Herbal Kombucha and Vinegars

Fermenting herbal kombucha and vinegars is a transformative process that not only preserves the herbs' beneficial properties but also enhances their bioavailability. This section delves into the methods and specifics of fermenting herbs for medicinal kombucha and vinegars, providing you with the knowledge to create these potent remedies at home.

Herbal Kombucha Fermentation

1. **Starter Culture**: Begin with a SCOBY (Symbiotic Culture Of Bacteria and Yeast), which you can obtain from an existing batch of kombucha or purchase. Ensure the SCOBY is healthy and free from mold.

2. **Tea Base**: Brew a strong herbal tea as the base for your kombucha. Choose herbs based on their health benefits and flavors. For example, chamomile for relaxation or ginger for digestive health. Use purified water to avoid chlorine, which can harm the SCOBY, and organic herbs to avoid pesticides.

3. **Sugar**: Add organic sugar to the tea while it's still hot. The sugar is not for you; it's food for the SCOBY. Typically, use about 1 cup of sugar per gallon of tea. Stir until fully dissolved.

4. **Cooling**: Allow the sweetened herbal tea to cool to room temperature to avoid harming the SCOBY.

5. **Fermentation**: Transfer the cooled tea to a large glass jar, gently add the SCOBY, and cover with a breathable cloth secured with a rubber band. Store the jar in a warm, dark place (around 68-78°F) for 7-14 days. Taste periodically after the first week until it reaches your desired level of tartness.

6. **Bottling**: Once fermented, carefully remove the SCOBY (save it for your next batch) and bottle the kombucha. For added flavor, you can introduce more herbs during this secondary fermentation phase. Seal the bottles and leave them at room temperature for 2-3 days to build carbonation, then refrigerate.

Herbal Vinegars

1. **Choosing Your Vinegar**: Start with a high-quality apple cider vinegar or white wine vinegar for the best medicinal properties. Ensure it's unpasteurized and contains the "mother" to benefit from its full probiotic potential.

2. **Herb Selection**: Select herbs that are known for their health benefits, such as rosemary for its cognitive support or garlic for its immune-boosting properties. Fresh herbs are preferred for their vitality, but dried herbs can also be used.

3. **Preparation**: If using fresh herbs, gently bruise or chop them to expose more surface area. Fill a clean jar about halfway with herbs.

4. **Infusion**: Heat the vinegar until warm but not boiling (to preserve its natural enzymes) and pour it over the herbs, completely submerging them. Leave about an inch of space at the top of the jar.

5. **Sealing and Storing**: Seal the jar with a plastic lid or place parchment paper under a metal lid to prevent corrosion from the vinegar. Label the jar with the date and contents. Store the jar in a cool, dark place for 4-6 weeks, shaking it every few days to mix the herbs.

6. **Straining**: After the infusion period, strain the herbs from the vinegar using a cheesecloth or fine mesh strainer. Bottle the vinegar in clean, sterilized bottles. For added benefit, you can add a fresh sprig of the infused herb to the bottle.

7. **Usage**: Herbal vinegars can be used internally, diluted in water as a health tonic, or externally, as part of a skin care regimen or for wound care. Always dilute the vinegar to at least a 1:10 ratio with water before consuming or applying topically to avoid irritation.

By following these detailed steps, you can harness the ancient wisdom of fermentation to create herbal kombuchas and vinegars that not only taste delightful but also offer significant health benefits. Whether you're looking to boost your immune system, improve digestion, or simply enjoy a refreshing, homemade probiotic drink, these fermented herbal preparations are a valuable addition to your natural health toolkit.

11.2: Probiotic Remedies for Gut Health

Probiotic remedies are a cornerstone of maintaining and enhancing gut health, leveraging the power of beneficial bacteria to support the digestive system and overall wellness. The preparation of these remedies involves fermenting certain foods and herbs to increase their probiotic content, making them a potent ally in your health regimen. Here are detailed steps and considerations for creating your own probiotic remedies at home, focusing on two primary methods: lacto-fermentation of vegetables and milk fermentation for making kefir.

Lacto-Fermentation of Vegetables

1. **Select Your Vegetables**: Begin with organic, fresh vegetables. Cabbage, carrots, and cucumbers are excellent choices for beginners due to their ease of fermentation and palatability. Wash them thoroughly to remove any dirt or debris.

2. **Prepare the Brine**: A basic brine is made from water and salt. Use filtered water to avoid chlorine, which can inhibit fermentation, and non-iodized salt, as iodine can kill the beneficial bacteria. The ratio is generally 1-3 tablespoons of salt per quart of water, depending on the vegetable and your taste preference.

3. **Cut or Shred Vegetables**: Depending on the vegetable, you may wish to shred, slice, or leave them in large chunks. Smaller pieces tend to ferment faster due to the increased surface area.

4. **Pack the Vegetables**: Place the vegetables in a clean, airtight jar, leaving at least an inch of space at the top. Pour the brine over the vegetables until they are completely submerged. It's crucial that the vegetables stay below the brine to prevent mold growth.

5. **Seal and Store**: Close the jar with a lid that allows gases to escape, such as a fermentation airlock lid, or simply loosen the lid slightly to let gases out manually every day. Store the jar at room temperature, out of direct sunlight, for anywhere from 3 days to several weeks. The length of fermentation will depend on the vegetable and your taste preference.

6. **Taste and Refrigerate**: Begin tasting the vegetables after a few days. Once they've reached your desired level of sourness, tighten the lid and move them to the refrigerator. This slows the fermentation process, and the vegetables can be enjoyed for several months.

Milk Fermentation for Kefir

1. **Obtain Kefir Grains**: Kefir is made using kefir grains, which are a symbiotic culture of bacteria and yeasts. These can be obtained from health food stores or online, or from someone already making kefir.

2. **Prepare the Milk**: Use any kind of milk, but organic, full-fat versions are preferred for their nutritional content and taste. Pour the milk into a clean glass jar.

3. **Add the Kefir Grains**: For every quart of milk, add approximately 1 tablespoon of kefir grains.

4. **Ferment the Milk**: Cover the jar with a breathable material, such as a paper towel or a clean cloth, secured with a rubber band. This allows air to circulate while keeping out contaminants. Place the jar in a warm spot, away from direct sunlight, and let it ferment for 12 to 48 hours. The fermentation time will depend on the temperature and how thick you prefer your kefir.

5. **Strain and Store**: Once fermented to your liking, strain out the kefir grains using a plastic strainer (metal can react with the kefir grains). The kefir is now ready to drink, and the grains can be reused immediately for another batch. Store the kefir in the refrigerator.

6. **Maintenance of Kefir Grains**: To keep the grains healthy, ferment a new batch of kefir regularly. If you need a break, the grains can be stored in the refrigerator in fresh milk for up to a week.

By integrating these probiotic-rich foods into your diet, you can support your gut health, which in turn can enhance your immune system, improve digestion, and contribute to overall well-being. Remember, the key to successful fermentation is cleanliness, patience, and a bit of experimentation to find the flavors and textures that you enjoy the most.

Book 4: Remedies for Everyday Wellness

Chapter 12: Immune and Respiratory Health

12.1: Boosting Immunity Naturally

Elderberry Syrup

Beneficial effects

Elderberry syrup is renowned for its immune-boosting properties. Rich in antioxidants and vitamins that can help fight colds, influenza, and boost the overall immune system. Studies have shown that elderberry can reduce the severity and duration of cold and flu symptoms.

Portions

Makes approximately 16 ounces (2 cups) of syrup.

Preparation time

10 minutes

Cooking time

45 minutes to 1 hour

Ingredients

- 3/4 cup dried elderberries

- 3 cups water

- 1 teaspoon dried ginger root

- 1/2 teaspoon cinnamon powder

- 1/4 teaspoon ground cloves

- 1 cup raw honey

Instructions

1. Combine the dried elderberries, water, dried ginger root, cinnamon powder, and ground cloves in a medium saucepan.
2. Bring the mixture to a boil, then reduce the heat to low and simmer for 45 minutes to 1 hour, or until the liquid has reduced by almost half.
3. Remove from heat and let cool until it is safe to handle.
4. Mash the berries carefully using a spoon or a potato masher to release any remaining juice.
5. Strain the mixture through a fine mesh strainer or cheesecloth into a large bowl. Press or squeeze the berries to extract as much liquid as possible.
6. Discard the solids and allow the liquid to cool to lukewarm.
7. Once the liquid is no longer hot, add the raw honey and stir until well combined.
8. Pour the syrup into a sterilized glass bottle or jar.

Variations

- For a vegan version, substitute the honey with maple syrup or agave nectar.

- Add a tablespoon of fresh lemon juice for additional vitamin C and a tangy flavor.

- Incorporate other immune-boosting herbs like echinacea or astragalus during the simmering process for added benefits.

Storage tips

Store the elderberry syrup in a sealed glass jar or bottle in the refrigerator. It will keep for up to 2-3 months. For longer storage, the syrup can be frozen in an ice cube tray and then transferred to a freezer bag, thawing individual cubes as needed.

Tips for allergens

If you are allergic to any of the ingredients, they can be omitted or substituted. For example, if you are allergic to honey, use the suggested vegan alternatives. Always ensure that you source high-quality, organic ingredients to minimize the risk of contaminants.

Garlic and Honey Tonic

Beneficial effects

Garlic and honey tonic is renowned for its immune-boosting properties. Garlic, with its natural antibiotic, antiviral, and antifungal qualities, helps to ward off and fight infections. Honey, on the other hand, acts as a soothing agent and antioxidant, providing support for the immune system and aiding in the healing process. Together, they create a powerful tonic that can help to prevent colds, reduce inflammation, and promote overall health.

Portions

Makes about 1 cup

Preparation time

10 minutes

Ingredients

- 1 cup of raw honey

- 10-12 cloves of fresh garlic, peeled and finely minced or crushed

Instructions

1. Begin by selecting a high-quality, raw honey, which retains more of its natural healing properties due to minimal processing.
2. Peel 10-12 cloves of fresh garlic. The fresher the garlic, the more potent its medicinal qualities, so choose bulbs that are firm and have tight, dry skins.
3. Finely mince or crush the garlic cloves. Crushing garlic releases allicin, its primary active compound, which is responsible for many of its health benefits. Use a garlic press or the flat side of a knife to effectively crush the cloves.
4. In a clean, dry jar, combine the minced or crushed garlic with 1 cup of raw honey. Stir the mixture thoroughly to ensure the garlic is evenly distributed throughout the honey.
5. Seal the jar tightly with a lid. Let the mixture sit at room temperature for 3-5 days to allow the ingredients to infuse. Each day, open the jar to stir the mixture and release any gases that may have built up.
6. After 3-5 days, the garlic and honey tonic is ready to use. For best results, consume 1-2 teaspoons of the tonic daily on an empty stomach.

Variations

- For an additional immune boost, add 1 teaspoon of freshly grated ginger or a pinch of cayenne pepper to the mixture.

- Incorporate 1 tablespoon of apple cider vinegar for its digestive benefits and to add a tangy flavor.

Storage tips

Store the garlic and honey tonic in a cool, dark place. The refrigerator is ideal, especially after opening, to help preserve its freshness and potency. Properly stored, the tonic can last up to a month or longer.

Tips for allergens

Individuals with allergies to pollen or bee products should proceed with caution when using raw honey. As an alternative, pure maple syrup can be used, although the medicinal properties will differ.

Echinacea Tea

Beneficial effects

Echinacea tea is renowned for its ability to boost the immune system, potentially reducing the duration and severity of colds and other respiratory infections. Its active compounds, including alkamides, polysaccharides, and glycoproteins, have been shown to enhance immune function, offering a natural way to support the body's defenses.

Portions

Makes approximately 2 cups

Preparation time

5 minutes

Cooking time

15 minutes

Ingredients

- 1 tablespoon dried Echinacea purpurea (leaves, flowers, and/or roots)

- 2 cups boiling water

- Honey or lemon (optional, for taste)

Instructions

1. Boil 2 cups of water in a medium-sized pot.
2. Measure 1 tablespoon of dried Echinacea and add it to the boiling water.
3. Reduce the heat and let it simmer for 15 minutes. This slow simmering process helps to extract the beneficial compounds from the Echinacea.
4. After 15 minutes, remove the pot from the heat.
5. Strain the tea into a cup or mug, removing the Echinacea solids.
6. If desired, add honey or lemon to taste. Honey can soothe a sore throat, while lemon can add a refreshing flavor and vitamin C.
7. Enjoy the tea warm for the best therapeutic effect.

Variations

- For a stronger immune boost, add a slice of fresh ginger or a clove of garlic while simmering.

- Combine with peppermint leaves or a cinnamon stick during the simmering process for additional flavor and benefits.

Storage tips

Echinacea tea is best enjoyed fresh but can be stored in the refrigerator for up to 2 days. Ensure it's stored in a sealed container to maintain its beneficial properties.

Tips for allergens

Individuals with allergies to plants in the daisy family, such as chamomile or ragweed, should proceed with caution when trying Echinacea for the first time due to potential cross-reactivity.

12.2. Remedies for Coughs, Sore Throats, and Congestion

Ginger Lemon Honey Tea

Beneficial effects

Ginger Lemon Honey Tea is a soothing remedy known for its anti-inflammatory, antioxidant, and antimicrobial properties, making it an excellent choice for relieving symptoms of coughs, sore throats, and congestion. Ginger helps to reduce inflammation and nausea, lemon boosts the immune system with vitamin C, and honey provides a soothing effect for sore throats while also acting as a natural cough suppressant.

Portions

Makes 2 servings

Preparation time

5 minutes

Cooking time

10 minutes

Ingredients

- 1 inch fresh ginger root, thinly sliced

- 2 cups water

- 1 lemon, juiced

- 2 tablespoons raw honey

Instructions

1. Begin by thoroughly washing the ginger root to remove any dirt or impurities. There's no need to peel the ginger, as the skin contains additional nutrients.
2. Thinly slice the ginger root to maximize the surface area exposed to the water, which helps to extract more of its beneficial compounds.
3. In a small saucepan, bring 2 cups of water to a boil. Add the sliced ginger to the boiling water.
4. Reduce the heat to a simmer and allow the ginger to steep in the water for about 10 minutes. This slow simmering process helps to infuse the water with the ginger's active compounds.
5. After simmering, remove the saucepan from the heat. Strain the ginger pieces from the water and pour the hot ginger-infused water into two mugs.

6. Stir in the juice of one lemon into the mugs. The lemon not only adds a refreshing flavor but also contributes vitamin C, which is essential for immune support.
7. Add one tablespoon of raw honey to each mug and stir well until the honey is fully dissolved. The honey acts as a natural sweetener and provides soothing relief for sore throats.
8. Serve the tea warm for immediate relief from cough, sore throat, and congestion symptoms.

Variations

- For an extra immune boost, add a pinch of cayenne pepper or turmeric to the tea while it simmers.

- Incorporate a cinnamon stick or a few cloves during the simmering process for added flavor and additional antimicrobial benefits.

Storage tips

If you have leftover tea, allow it to cool to room temperature before storing it in a sealed container in the refrigerator. Consume within 24 hours for best results. Reheat gently on the stove or in the microwave before drinking.

Tips for allergens

For those with allergies to honey, substitute it with maple syrup or agave nectar to maintain the soothing and sweet properties of the tea without triggering an allergic reaction.

Peppermint Steam Inhalation

Beneficial effects

Peppermint steam inhalation is a traditional remedy known for its soothing effects on the respiratory system. It can help alleviate symptoms of coughs, sore throats, and congestion by opening nasal passages, reducing inflammation, and providing antimicrobial benefits. The menthol in peppermint acts as a natural expectorant, promoting the clearance of mucus from the airways and making breathing easier. Additionally, the warmth of the steam can moisten dry, irritated throat tissues, providing immediate relief.

Ingredients

- 3-4 cups of water

- 10-15 fresh peppermint leaves or 3-5 drops of peppermint essential oil

Instructions

1. Bring 3-4 cups of water to a boil in a medium-sized pot. The amount of water used should be enough to produce steam for 5-10 minutes.
2. While the water is heating, thoroughly wash the peppermint leaves to remove any dirt or impurities. If using peppermint essential oil, ensure it is 100% pure and therapeutic grade for the best medicinal properties.

3. Once the water reaches a rolling boil, remove the pot from the heat. If using fresh peppermint leaves, tear or crush them slightly with your hands to release the essential oils, then add them to the hot water. If using peppermint essential oil, add 3-5 drops directly to the water instead.
4. Lean over the pot at a safe distance, ensuring not to get too close to avoid burns from the steam. Drape a large towel over your head and the pot, creating a tent that traps the steam.
5. Inhale the peppermint-infused steam deeply for 5-10 minutes, or as long as the steam is visibly rising. Take slow, deep breaths through your nose and out through your mouth to maximize the inhalation of the therapeutic properties.
6. After completing the inhalation, gently pat your face dry with a towel. Drink a glass of water to stay hydrated.

Variations

- For additional respiratory benefits, add a teaspoon of eucalyptus leaves or 2-3 drops of eucalyptus essential oil to the boiling water along with the peppermint.

- To enhance relaxation and further soothe sore throats, mix in a tablespoon of chamomile flowers or 2-3 drops of chamomile essential oil.

Storage tips

Fresh peppermint leaves should be stored in the refrigerator in a damp paper towel and a plastic bag for up to a week. Peppermint essential oil should be kept in a cool, dark place to maintain its potency.

Tips for allergens

Individuals with allergies to menthol or other compounds in peppermint should proceed with caution. A patch test with diluted peppermint oil on the skin can help determine sensitivity. If allergic, consider substituting with eucalyptus or chamomile, which also offer respiratory benefits without the use of peppermint.

Thyme and Honey Cough Syrup

Beneficial effects

Thyme and honey cough syrup is a traditional remedy known for its antimicrobial and soothing properties. Thyme contains compounds like thymol and carvacrol, which have been shown to possess antibacterial and antiviral activities, making it effective in treating coughs and sore throats. Honey, on the other hand, acts as a natural demulcent, providing a protective film over irritated mucous membranes, and has been scientifically proven to help reduce cough frequency and improve sleep quality in children with upper respiratory infections.

Portions	Cooking time
Makes about 1 cup	20 minutes

Preparation time	Ingredients
5 minutes	- 2 tablespoons of dried thyme leaves

- 1 cup of water   - 1 cup of raw honey

Instructions

1. Begin by boiling 1 cup of water in a small saucepan.
2. Once the water reaches a rolling boil, add 2 tablespoons of dried thyme leaves.
3. Reduce the heat to low and let the thyme simmer for 15 minutes. This process allows the water to become infused with the thyme's essential oils and compounds.
4. After simmering, remove the saucepan from the heat and carefully strain the thyme-infused water through a fine mesh strainer or cheesecloth into a heat-resistant bowl or measuring cup, pressing on the thyme leaves to extract as much liquid as possible. Discard the thyme leaves.
5. While the thyme infusion is still warm (but not hot), add 1 cup of raw honey to the bowl.
6. Stir the mixture gently until the honey is completely dissolved into the thyme infusion.
7. Once the honey is fully integrated, pour the syrup into a clean, dry glass jar with a tight-fitting lid.

Variations

- For added benefits, include a tablespoon of freshly squeezed lemon juice to the syrup, which can provide vitamin C and further soothe the throat.

- Incorporate a pinch of ground ginger or cinnamon for additional antimicrobial properties and to enhance the flavor.

Storage tips

Store the thyme and honey cough syrup in the refrigerator for up to 3 months. Ensure the jar is sealed tightly after each use to maintain freshness and prevent contamination.

Tips for allergens

Individuals with allergies to bee products should proceed with caution when using honey. As an alternative, maple syrup can be used, although the medicinal properties and flavor profile will differ.

Chapter 13: Stress, Sleep, and Mental Health

13.1: Managing Stress and Anxiety

Chamomile Lavender Tea

Beneficial effects

Chamomile Lavender Tea is renowned for its calming and soothing properties, making it an ideal beverage for reducing stress and anxiety. Chamomile is known for its ability to relax the mind and body, improve sleep quality, and reduce inflammation. Lavender adds to the calming effect with its own stress-relieving and anti-anxiety properties. Together, they create a powerful blend that can help soothe the nervous system, promoting a sense of calm and well-being.

Portions

Makes 2 servings

Preparation time

5 minutes

Cooking time

10 minutes

Ingredients

- 2 tablespoons dried chamomile flowers

- 1 tablespoon dried lavender buds

- 2 cups boiling water

- Honey or lemon (optional, for taste)

Instructions

1. Boil 2 cups of water in a kettle or a pot.
2. While the water is boiling, measure out 2 tablespoons of dried chamomile flowers and 1 tablespoon of dried lavender buds.
3. Place the chamomile and lavender in a tea infuser or directly into a teapot.
4. Once the water has reached a rolling boil, pour it over the chamomile and lavender in the teapot.
5. Cover the teapot and allow the tea to steep for 5-7 minutes, depending on your taste preference. The longer it steeps, the stronger the flavor and therapeutic effects.
6. After steeping, remove the tea infuser or strain the tea to remove the chamomile flowers and lavender buds.
7. Serve the tea in cups. If desired, add honey or a squeeze of lemon to enhance the flavor.
8. Enjoy the tea while it's warm, taking slow sips and allowing the calming aroma to soothe your senses.

Variations

- For a cooler, refreshing version, allow the tea to cool and serve it over ice.

- Add a cinnamon stick or a few slices of fresh ginger to the boiling water for additional flavor and health benefits.

- Mix in a teaspoon of mint leaves for a refreshing twist and added digestive benefits.

Storage tips

The dried chamomile flowers and lavender buds should be stored in airtight containers away from direct sunlight and moisture to preserve their potency and flavor. The prepared tea can be stored in the refrigerator for up to 2 days in a sealed container.

Tips for allergens

Individuals with allergies to plants in the daisy family, such as chamomile, should proceed with caution. As an alternative, consider using solely lavender or a different calming herb like lemon balm that does not belong to the daisy family.

Valerian Root Tincture

Beneficial effects

Valerian root tincture is widely recognized for its ability to soothe anxiety and promote restful sleep. The compounds within valerian, such as valerenic acid and isovaleric acid, interact with the gamma-aminobutyric acid (GABA) receptor in the brain, a mechanism similar to that of anxiety medications, but in a natural form. This interaction helps to calm the nervous system, making it easier to fall asleep and manage stress levels effectively.

Portions

Makes about 1 pint

Preparation time

10 minutes (plus 4-6 weeks for infusing)

Ingredients

- 4 ounces dried valerian root

- 1 pint (16 ounces) high-proof alcohol (vodka or brandy, at least 80 proof)

Instructions

1. Begin by sourcing high-quality, organic dried valerian root to ensure the potency and safety of your tincture.
2. Place the dried valerian root in a clean, dry jar. A pint-sized mason jar works well for this purpose.
3. Pour the high-proof alcohol over the valerian root, ensuring that the roots are completely submerged. If necessary, add a bit more alcohol to cover the roots by at least an inch to account for absorption.
4. Seal the jar tightly with a lid. Label the jar with the date and contents for future reference.
5. Store the jar in a cool, dark place, such as a cupboard or pantry, away from direct sunlight and heat sources.
6. Shake the jar gently every day to mix the contents and facilitate the extraction process.
7. Allow the mixture to infuse for 4-6 weeks. The longer it infuses, the stronger the tincture will be.
8. After the infusion period, strain the tincture through a fine mesh strainer or cheesecloth into another clean, dry jar or bottle. Squeeze or press the valerian root to extract as much liquid as possible.
9. Discard the used valerian root and transfer the strained tincture into dark glass dropper bottles for easy use.

Variations

- For those sensitive to alcohol, glycerin can be used as a non-alcoholic alternative, though the extraction process may differ slightly and the shelf life will be shorter.

- Combine with other calming herbs such as chamomile or lavender to enhance the soothing effects.

Storage tips

Store the valerian root tincture in a cool, dark place. Dark glass bottles help to preserve the tincture's potency by protecting it from light. Properly stored, the tincture can last for several years.

Tips for allergens

For individuals with allergies to alcohol, using a glycerin-based tincture provides a viable alternative, though it's important to ensure the glycerin is derived from sources you are not allergic to.

13.2: Overcoming Insomnia Remedies

Passionflower Sleep Tea

Beneficial effects

Passionflower Sleep Tea is recognized for its calming and sedative properties, making it an excellent natural remedy for insomnia and anxiety. The active compounds in passionflower, including flavonoids and alkaloids, interact with the brain's GABA receptors to reduce brain activity, which helps to promote relaxation and improve sleep quality. This gentle herbal tea can be a beneficial part of a nightly routine for those looking to ease their mind and encourage a restful night's sleep without the use of pharmaceutical sleep aids.

Portions

Makes 2 servings

Preparation time

5 minutes

Cooking time

10 minutes

Ingredients

- 2 teaspoons dried passionflower leaves

- 2 cups boiling water

- Honey or lemon (optional, for taste)

Instructions

1. Bring 2 cups of water to a rolling boil in a medium-sized pot or kettle.
2. Place 2 teaspoons of dried passionflower leaves into a tea infuser or directly into the pot.
3. Once the water has reached a boil, pour it over the passionflower leaves, ensuring they are fully submerged.
4. Cover the pot or kettle and allow the tea to steep for 8-10 minutes. The longer steeping time allows for the full extraction of the passionflower's active compounds.

5. After steeping, remove the tea infuser or strain the tea to remove the loose leaves.
6. If desired, add honey or a squeeze of lemon to the tea for flavor. Honey can provide a soothing sweetness, while lemon adds a refreshing tang and vitamin C.
7. Divide the tea into two cups, and enjoy it warm before bedtime to help prepare your body and mind for sleep.

Variations

- For additional relaxation benefits, blend passionflower with other calming herbs such as chamomile or lavender. Use 1 teaspoon of passionflower and 1 teaspoon of your chosen herb per serving.

- To enhance the sleep-promoting effects, include a teaspoon of valerian root to the infusion, but be mindful that valerian can have a strong taste.

- For a cooler, more refreshing nighttime beverage during warmer months, allow the tea to cool and serve it over ice.

Storage tips

Store dried passionflower leaves in an airtight container away from direct sunlight and moisture to maintain their potency and freshness. The dried herb should retain its effectiveness for up to a year if stored properly.

Tips for allergens

For individuals with allergies to specific herbs, ensure that passionflower is suitable for your use by consulting with a healthcare provider. If adding other herbs to the tea, select those you know are safe for your consumption.

Herbal Pillow Spray

Beneficial effects

Herbal Pillow Spray combines the calming and sleep-promoting properties of essential oils to create a restful environment conducive to sleep. Lavender essential oil is renowned for its ability to reduce anxiety and induce sleep, while chamomile essential oil offers soothing and relaxing effects. Spraying this blend on your pillow can help ease the mind, reduce stress, and improve the quality of sleep by creating a peaceful and aromatic atmosphere.

Ingredients

- 3 ounces distilled water

- 1 ounce witch hazel or vodka (as a preservative and to help disperse the oil in water)

- 20 drops lavender essential oil

- 10 drops chamomile essential oil

- Small spray bottle (4-ounce capacity)

Instructions

1. Start by ensuring your spray bottle is clean and dry. A 4-ounce capacity bottle is ideal for this recipe, providing enough space for shaking the mixture before each use.
2. Measure 3 ounces of distilled water and pour it into the spray bottle. Distilled water is recommended to prevent any potential bacterial growth that can occur with tap water.
3. Add 1 ounce of witch hazel or vodka to the bottle. This acts as a preservative and helps to evenly disperse the essential oils throughout the water, preventing them from separating.
4. Carefully add 20 drops of lavender essential oil to the mixture. Lavender oil is the primary calming agent in this spray, known for its sleep-inducing and stress-relieving properties.
5. Incorporate 10 drops of chamomile essential oil. Chamomile enhances the calming effects of lavender, promoting deeper relaxation and sleep.
6. Secure the lid on the spray bottle and shake well for about 15-20 seconds to ensure the oils are thoroughly mixed with the water and witch hazel or vodka.
7. To use, gently shake the bottle and lightly spray onto your pillow and bedding a few minutes before going to bed. This allows the scent to disperse and not be too overwhelming.
8. Store the bottle in a cool, dark place when not in use to preserve the essential oils' therapeutic properties.

Variations

- For additional sleep benefits, consider adding 5 drops of vetiver or bergamot essential oil to the mix. Vetiver is known for its grounding properties, while bergamot can help alleviate stress and anxiety.

- If you prefer a slightly different scent, substitute Roman chamomile essential oil with sweet orange or ylang-ylang essential oil for a more personalized aroma that still promotes relaxation and sleep.

Storage tips

Keep the herbal pillow spray in a cool, dark place to maintain the efficacy of the essential oils. Avoid exposing the bottle to direct sunlight or heat, as this can degrade the oils and reduce the spray's effectiveness. The mixture should remain potent for up to 6 months if stored properly.

Tips for allergens

Individuals with sensitivities to specific essential oils should perform a patch test before using the spray extensively. Apply a small amount of the diluted essential oil (as used in the spray) to the skin and wait 24 hours to check for any adverse reactions. If irritation occurs, consider reducing the concentration of essential oils or substituting them with more suitable alternatives.

Lavender Chamomile Bath Soak

Beneficial effects

The Lavender Chamomile Bath Soak combines the calming and soothing properties of lavender and chamomile, making it an excellent remedy for overcoming insomnia and promoting relaxation before bedtime. Lavender is well-known for its ability to decrease anxiety and induce sleep by impacting the nervous system directly, while chamomile has been used for centuries to help with sleeplessness, stress, and anxiety. Together, they create a powerful blend that can help ease the mind, relax the muscles, and prepare the body for a restful night's sleep.

Ingredients

- 1/2 cup dried chamomile flowers

- 1/2 cup dried lavender buds

- 1 cup Epsom salt

- 1/2 cup baking soda

- Optional: A few drops of lavender essential oil for enhanced aromatic benefits

Instructions

1. Begin by mixing the dried chamomile flowers and dried lavender buds in a large bowl. Ensure that both herbs are thoroughly combined.
2. Add 1 cup of Epsom salt to the bowl with the herbs. Epsom salt is rich in magnesium, which is known for its muscle-relaxing and stress-reducing properties.
3. Incorporate 1/2 cup of baking soda to the mixture. Baking soda helps to soften the water and can soothe irritated skin, enhancing the relaxing effects of the bath soak.
4. If desired, add a few drops of lavender essential oil to the mixture for an extra aromatic experience. Lavender essential oil not only strengthens the soak's calming scent but also contributes additional stress-relieving benefits.
5. Stir all the ingredients until they are well mixed.
6. To use, pour the entire mixture into a warm bath as it's filling.
7. Soak in the bath for at least 20 minutes, allowing the herbs, Epsom salt, and baking soda to work their magic. For the best results, engage in this relaxing ritual about an hour before bedtime.
8. After the bath, wrap yourself in a warm towel or robe and proceed with your nighttime routine, aiming to go to bed shortly after to maximize the benefits of the soak.

Variations

- For a more moisturizing soak, add 1/4 cup of coconut milk powder or oatmeal to the mixture. Both ingredients are known for their skin-soothing and moisturizing properties.

- Incorporate a tablespoon of dried rose petals for an added floral scent and a touch of luxury to your bath experience.

- For those who prefer a salt-free option, simply omit the Epsom salt and increase the amounts of chamomile and lavender.

Storage tips

Store the unused bath soak mixture in an airtight container, away from direct sunlight and moisture, to preserve its freshness and potency. It can be kept for up to 6 months if stored properly.

Tips for allergens

Individuals with allergies to chamomile or lavender should perform a patch test before using the bath soak or consider substituting these with other non-allergenic herbs like rose petals or calendula, which also offer calming properties.

Chapter 14: Skin and Hair Care

14.1: Healing Burns, Cuts, and Bruises

Aloe Vera Gel for Burns

Beneficial effects

Aloe Vera Gel for Burns harnesses the natural soothing and anti-inflammatory properties of aloe vera, making it an excellent remedy for treating minor burns and skin irritations. Aloe vera contains compounds such as glycoproteins and polysaccharides that help reduce pain and inflammation while promoting skin healing and hydration. Its cooling effect provides immediate relief for discomfort caused by burns.

Ingredients

- 1 large aloe vera leaf

- 1 teaspoon vitamin E oil (optional, for added skin healing and preservation)

- 1/2 teaspoon pure lavender essential oil (optional, for soothing aroma and enhanced skin healing properties)

Instructions

1. Start by selecting a large, healthy aloe vera leaf from an aloe vera plant. Choose one that is plump and green, indicating it is full of gel.
2. Rinse the leaf under cool running water to clean off any dirt or debris. Pat it dry with a clean towel.
3. Using a sharp knife, carefully slice off the serrated edges of the leaf on both sides. This makes it easier to access the gel inside.
4. Next, slice the leaf open lengthwise from the top down. You should now be able to see the clear aloe vera gel inside.
5. With a spoon, gently scoop out the gel into a clean bowl. Try to get as much gel as possible without including any of the yellowish aloe latex that is close to the leaf skin, as this can be irritating to some skin types.
6. If you're adding vitamin E oil and lavender essential oil for their additional skin healing benefits and preservation, add them to the bowl now.
7. Using a blender or a hand mixer, blend the aloe vera gel and oils together for about 30 seconds to a minute, until the mixture is smooth and slightly frothy.
8. Pour the blended gel into a clean, airtight container. If you have not added the optional oils, the gel will be quite watery.
9. Label the container with the date and contents.

Variations

- For an extra cooling effect, store the aloe vera gel in the refrigerator before applying to the burn.

- Mix the aloe vera gel with a few drops of tea tree oil for its natural antiseptic properties, beneficial for preventing infection in minor burns.

Storage tips

Store the aloe vera gel in an airtight container in the refrigerator for up to one week. If you've added vitamin E and lavender oil, the gel can last up to two weeks due to their natural preservative properties. For longer storage, freeze the gel in an ice cube tray and transfer the frozen cubes to a freezer bag, keeping them frozen until needed.

Tips for allergens

Individuals with sensitive skin or allergies to aloe vera should perform a patch test on a small area of skin before applying it to a larger burn area. Substitute aloe vera with coconut oil or honey for their soothing and healing properties if aloe vera is not suitable.

Calendula Salve for Cuts

Beneficial effects

Calendula Salve is renowned for its potent anti-inflammatory, antifungal, and antimicrobial properties, making it an excellent natural remedy for healing cuts, scrapes, and various skin irritations. The active compounds in calendula, such as flavonoids and saponins, contribute to its ability to speed up wound healing by promoting cell repair and growth, reducing inflammation, and fighting off infection. This gentle yet effective salve can be a go-to solution for skin care in a survival apothecary setting, offering a soothing and protective barrier for damaged skin.

Portions

Makes approximately 4 ounces (120 ml) of salve

Preparation time

15 minutes

Cooking time

1 hour

Ingredients

- 1 cup of dried calendula petals

- 1 cup of coconut oil (or olive oil as an alternative)

- 1/4 cup of beeswax pellets

- Optional: 10-15 drops of lavender essential oil for added antimicrobial and soothing properties

Instructions

1. Begin by infusing the oil with dried calendula petals. Place the petals in a double boiler, and cover them with the coconut oil. If you don't have a double boiler, you can use a heat-safe bowl over a pot of simmering water.
2. Allow the calendula and oil mixture to infuse over low heat for about 1-2 hours. Ensure the heat is low enough to avoid frying the petals, aiming for a gentle simmer at most. Stir occasionally to ensure even infusion.
3. After the infusion period, carefully strain the oil through a fine mesh strainer or cheesecloth into a clean bowl or jar, removing all the calendula petals. Squeeze or press the petals to extract as much oil as possible.
4. Clean the double boiler or bowl, then return the strained oil to it. Add the beeswax pellets to the oil.
5. Heat the mixture over low heat, stirring continuously until the beeswax is completely melted and combined with the oil, creating a smooth mixture.
6. Remove from heat. If using, add the lavender essential oil to the mixture at this point and stir well to ensure it's evenly distributed throughout the salve.
7. Carefully pour the liquid salve into small tins or jars. Allow the salve to cool and solidify at room temperature. This may take several hours.
8. Once solidified, seal the containers with lids to prevent contamination and preserve the salve's properties.

Variations

- For extra healing properties, add a teaspoon of vitamin E oil to the mixture before pouring it into containers. Vitamin E can help improve the salve's shelf life and support skin healing.

- If calendula is not available, chamomile flowers can be used as a substitute for similar anti-inflammatory and soothing effects.

Storage tips

Store the calendula salve in a cool, dark place. If stored properly, the salve can last for up to a year. Over time, natural products may lose some potency, so it's best to make small batches that can be used within a few months.

Tips for allergens

For those with allergies to beeswax, a plant-based wax like candelilla wax can be used as an alternative. Note that the consistency may vary, so adjustments to the amount of wax may be needed. Always perform a patch test before applying a new product extensively, especially on damaged skin.

Arnica Balm for Bruises

Beneficial effects

Arnica balm is renowned for its anti-inflammatory and analgesic properties, making it an effective natural remedy for treating bruises, reducing swelling, and alleviating pain. Arnica montana, the plant from which the balm is made, contains compounds such as helenalin and flavonoids that contribute to its therapeutic effects. These compounds help to stimulate circulation, reduce inflammation, and accelerate the healing of tissues, making arnica balm a must-have in any natural first aid kit.

Ingredients

- 1/4 cup arnica-infused oil

- 1/4 cup coconut oil

- 1/4 cup shea butter

- 1/4 cup beeswax pellets

- 10 drops lavender essential oil (optional for additional pain relief and scent)

- Small glass jars or metal tins for storage

Instructions

1. Begin by preparing a double boiler. Fill a pot with a few inches of water and place it on the stove over medium heat. Position a heat-safe glass bowl or smaller pot on top of the pot, ensuring the bottom doesn't touch the water.
2. Add the beeswax pellets to the bowl and allow them to melt slowly, stirring occasionally with a heat-resistant spatula or spoon.
3. Once the beeswax is completely melted, add the arnica-infused oil, coconut oil, and shea butter to the bowl. Stir the mixture gently until all the ingredients are melted and well combined.
4. Remove the bowl from the heat. If using, add the lavender essential oil to the mixture and stir well to ensure even distribution.
5. Carefully pour the liquid balm into small glass jars or metal tins. Allow the balm to cool and solidify at room temperature, which may take several hours. Avoid moving the containers until the balm is fully set to prevent any spills or uneven surfaces.
6. Once cooled and solidified, secure the lids on the containers to keep the balm protected from light and air exposure.

Variations

- For extra healing properties, consider adding vitamin E oil as an antioxidant and skin protector. Add about 1/2 teaspoon to the mixture after removing it from the heat.

- If you prefer a softer balm, reduce the amount of beeswax by a few pellets. For a firmer balm, especially in warmer climates, add an additional tablespoon of beeswax.

Storage tips

Store the arnica balm in a cool, dark place to preserve its potency. If stored properly, the balm can last for up to a year. Over time, natural products may lose some of their effectiveness, so it's best to make small batches that can be used within a few months.

Tips for allergens

Individuals with sensitivity to arnica, daisy family plants, or any other ingredients should perform a patch test before widespread use. To test, apply a small amount of the balm to the inside of your wrist and wait 24 hours to see if there is any adverse reaction. If irritation occurs, discontinue use immediately.

14.2: Remedies for Acne and Dry Skin

Tea Tree Oil and Aloe Vera Gel

Beneficial effects

Tea Tree Oil and Aloe Vera Gel combines the antimicrobial properties of tea tree oil with the soothing, hydrating effects of aloe vera. This natural remedy is particularly effective for treating acne and dry skin. Tea tree oil's ability to combat bacteria and reduce inflammation makes it a powerful ingredient for clearing up acne, while aloe vera's moisturizing and healing properties help to soothe and hydrate the skin, promoting a healthy skin barrier.

Ingredients

- 1/4 cup pure aloe vera gel

- 10 drops of tea tree essential oil

- 1 teaspoon of vitamin E oil (optional, for added skin nourishment and preservation)

- Small, clean, and dry container with lid

Instructions

1. Start by ensuring your aloe vera gel is pure and free from added colors, fragrances, or alcohol, which can irritate sensitive skin.
2. In a clean mixing bowl, combine 1/4 cup of aloe vera gel with 10 drops of tea tree essential oil. If using, add 1 teaspoon of vitamin E oil to the mixture. Vitamin E oil acts as an antioxidant that can extend the shelf life of your gel and provide additional benefits to the skin.
3. Using a small whisk or fork, stir the mixture thoroughly for about a minute to ensure the tea tree oil is evenly distributed throughout the aloe vera gel.
4. Carefully transfer the mixture into your clean, dry container. A small funnel can be helpful to avoid spills.
5. Secure the lid on the container and label it with the date and contents.

Variations

- For an extra cooling effect, store the gel in the refrigerator. The coolness can help soothe inflamed skin further.

- If you have particularly sensitive skin, reduce the amount of tea tree oil to 5 drops to minimize the risk of irritation.

- For added hydration, mix in a few drops of jojoba oil or sweet almond oil, which can help to further moisturize the skin without clogging pores.

Storage tips

Keep the Tea Tree Oil and Aloe Vera Gel in a cool, dark place, ideally in the refrigerator, to maintain its freshness and potency. The gel should be used within 1 month, especially if not including vitamin E oil as a preservative.

Tips for allergens

Individuals with sensitive skin or allergies to tea tree oil should perform a patch test before applying the gel extensively. Apply a small amount of the gel to the inside of your wrist and wait 24 hours to check for any adverse reaction. If irritation occurs, consider omitting the tea tree oil and using only the aloe vera gel, which is generally well-tolerated by sensitive skin types.

Honey and Oatmeal Face Mask

Beneficial effects

The Honey and Oatmeal Face Mask is a gentle, nourishing remedy ideal for soothing acne-prone and dry skin. Honey, with its natural antibacterial and anti-inflammatory properties, helps to cleanse the skin and reduce acne breakouts without stripping the skin of its natural oils. Oatmeal, on the other hand, acts as a natural exfoliant, removing dead skin cells, soothing irritation, and improving skin hydration. Together, they create a mask that not only moisturizes and heals but also leaves the skin feeling soft and rejuvenated.

Portions

This recipe yields enough for 2 applications.

Preparation time

10 minutes

Cooking time

No cooking required

Ingredients

- 1/2 cup finely ground oatmeal

- 2 tablespoons raw honey, preferably organic

- 1/4 cup warm water

- Optional: 1 teaspoon of lemon juice for additional cleansing properties

Instructions

1. Start by grinding the oatmeal in a food processor or blender until it reaches a fine powder consistency.
2. In a clean mixing bowl, combine the finely ground oatmeal with the raw honey. Mix these ingredients until they form a paste.

3. Gradually add the warm water to the oatmeal and honey mixture, stirring continuously until the mixture is smooth and fully combined. If the mixture is too thick, add a little more water until you achieve the desired consistency.
4. If opting to use lemon juice for its added benefits, such as brightening and helping to remove excess oil, mix in the teaspoon of lemon juice thoroughly.
5. Apply the mask to a clean, dry face using gentle, circular motions. Be careful to avoid the area around the eyes.
6. Allow the mask to sit on your skin for about 10-15 minutes. During this time, the mask will begin to dry slightly.
7. Rinse the mask off with lukewarm water, using gentle circular motions to provide additional exfoliation.
8. Pat your face dry with a soft, clean towel. Follow up with your regular moisturizer to lock in hydration.

Variations

- For extra moisturizing properties, add a teaspoon of coconut oil to the mixture. This is especially beneficial for very dry or flaky skin.

- Incorporate a few drops of tea tree oil for enhanced antibacterial benefits, making it more effective against acne-prone skin.

- To target hyperpigmentation, add a teaspoon of turmeric powder to the mix. Turmeric is known for its anti-inflammatory and skin-brightening properties.

Storage tips

It's best to prepare the Honey and Oatmeal Face Mask fresh for each use to ensure its potency and prevent spoilage. However, if you have leftovers, you can store the mixture in an airtight container in the refrigerator for up to 2 days. Before reapplying, let the mask return to room temperature or slightly warm it for a more pleasant application.

Tips for allergens

Individuals with gluten sensitivities should ensure that the oatmeal used is certified gluten-free to avoid potential allergic reactions. Those with sensitivity to honey can substitute it with aloe vera gel for its soothing and hydrating properties. Always perform a patch test on a small area of your skin before applying new ingredients to your entire face.

Chapter 15. Women's and Children's Health

15.1: Menstrual and Menopausal Support

Red Clover Infusion

Beneficial effects

Red Clover Infusion is celebrated for its potential to alleviate symptoms associated with menopause and menstrual discomfort. Rich in isoflavones, a type of phytoestrogen, red clover acts similarly to estrogen in the body, which can help balance hormone levels and mitigate symptoms such as hot flashes, night sweats, and mood fluctuations. Additionally, its anti-inflammatory properties may provide relief from menstrual cramps and bloating.

Portions

Makes about 4 cups

Preparation time

5 minutes

Cooking time

15 minutes

Ingredients

- 4 cups of water

- 1/4 cup dried red clover blossoms

- Optional: Honey or lemon to taste

Instructions

1. Bring 4 cups of water to a boil in a medium-sized saucepan.
2. Once the water is boiling, remove the saucepan from the heat.
3. Add 1/4 cup of dried red clover blossoms to the hot water. If using a tea infuser or tea bag, place the blossoms inside before adding them to the water.
4. Cover the saucepan with a lid and let the red clover blossoms steep for 10 to 15 minutes. The longer it steeps, the stronger the infusion will be.
5. After steeping, strain the red clover blossoms from the infusion using a fine mesh strainer or remove the tea infuser or tea bag.
6. If desired, add honey or lemon to the red clover infusion for flavor.
7. Serve the infusion warm, or allow it to cool and serve it chilled for a refreshing drink.

Variations

- For additional health benefits, consider adding a teaspoon of dried nettle leaves or raspberry leaf to the infusion during the steeping process.

- Mix in a cinnamon stick or a few slices of fresh ginger with the red clover blossoms for a warming, spicy flavor.

Storage tips

Store any leftover red clover infusion in a sealed glass container in the refrigerator for up to 2 days. Reheat gently on the stove or enjoy cold for a revitalizing drink.

Tips for allergens

Individuals with hormone-sensitive conditions should consult with a healthcare provider before consuming red clover due to its phytoestrogen content. Those allergic to plants in the Fabaceae family, such as clover, should avoid this infusion.

Black Cohosh Tea

Beneficial effects

Black Cohosh Tea is traditionally used to alleviate symptoms associated with menopause and menstruation, such as hot flashes, mood swings, and sleep disturbances. The active compounds in black cohosh, including triterpene glycosides, have been shown to have estrogen-like effects, helping to balance hormone levels and offer relief from menopausal and menstrual discomfort.

Portions

Makes 2 servings

Preparation time

5 minutes

Cooking time

10 minutes

Ingredients

- 1 teaspoon dried black cohosh root

- 2 cups water

- Honey or lemon to taste (optional)

Instructions

1. Bring 2 cups of water to a boil in a medium-sized pot.
2. Add 1 teaspoon of dried black cohosh root to the boiling water.
3. Reduce the heat to low and let the tea simmer for about 10 minutes. This allows the water to become infused with the properties of the black cohosh.
4. After simmering, remove the pot from the heat.
5. Strain the tea through a fine mesh strainer or cheesecloth into a teapot or directly into cups, discarding the used black cohosh root.
6. If desired, add honey or a squeeze of lemon to the tea for flavor. Honey can provide a soothing sweetness, while lemon adds a refreshing tang and vitamin C.
7. Serve the tea warm. For best results, drink one cup of black cohosh tea in the morning and another in the evening.

Variations

- To enhance the tea's benefits for menstrual support, consider adding a teaspoon of dried ginger to the boiling water along with the black cohosh. Ginger can help reduce menstrual cramps and inflammation.

- For additional flavor and calming effects, include a bag of chamomile tea while the black cohosh is simmering. Chamomile is known for its ability to reduce anxiety and promote relaxation.

Storage tips

Store any leftover tea in the refrigerator for up to 2 days. Reheat gently on the stove or enjoy cold. Keep dried black cohosh root in an airtight container in a cool, dark place to maintain its potency.

Tips for allergens

Individuals with allergies or sensitivities to aspirin or other salicylates should use caution when consuming black cohosh, as it may contain similar compounds. Always consult with a healthcare provider before adding new herbal teas to your regimen, especially if you are pregnant, nursing, or taking medication.

Dong Quai Tincture

Beneficial effects

Dong Quai Tincture is revered for its ability to support women's health, particularly in relieving symptoms associated with menstrual cycles and menopause. Dong Quai, often referred to as "female ginseng," contains compounds that may help in balancing hormones, reducing menstrual cramps, and alleviating menopausal symptoms such as hot flashes and mood swings. Its anti-inflammatory and analgesic properties can also contribute to its effectiveness in reducing pain and swelling.

Portions

Makes about 1 pint

Preparation time

10 minutes (plus 4-6 weeks for infusing)

Cooking time

No cooking required

Ingredients

- 4 ounces dried Dong Quai root, sliced or chopped

- 1 pint (16 ounces) high-proof alcohol (vodka or brandy, at least 80 proof)

Instructions

1. Begin by sourcing high-quality, organic dried Dong Quai root to ensure the potency and safety of your tincture.
2. Place the dried Dong Quai root in a clean, dry jar. A pint-sized mason jar is ideal for this purpose.
3. Pour the high-proof alcohol over the Dong Quai root, making sure that the roots are completely submerged. If necessary, add a bit more alcohol to cover the roots by at least an inch to account for absorption.
4. Seal the jar tightly with a lid. Label the jar with the date and contents for future reference.

5. Store the jar in a cool, dark place, such as a cupboard or pantry, away from direct sunlight and heat sources.
6. Shake the jar gently every day to mix the contents and facilitate the extraction process.
7. Allow the mixture to infuse for 4-6 weeks. The longer it infuses, the stronger the tincture will be.
8. After the infusion period, strain the tincture through a fine mesh strainer or cheesecloth into another clean, dry jar or bottle. Squeeze or press the Dong Quai root to extract as much liquid as possible.
9. Discard the used Dong Quai root and transfer the strained tincture into dark glass dropper bottles for easy use.

Variations

- For those sensitive to alcohol, glycerin can be used as a non-alcoholic alternative, though the extraction process may differ slightly and the shelf life will be shorter.

- Combine Dong Quai tincture with other herbal tinctures such as black cohosh or red clover to enhance the synergistic effects on menopausal symptoms.

Storage tips

Store the Dong Quai tincture in a cool, dark place. Dark glass bottles help to preserve the tincture's potency by protecting it from light. Properly stored, the tincture can last for several years.

Tips for allergens

For individuals with allergies to alcohol, using a glycerin-based tincture provides a viable alternative, though it's important to ensure the glycerin is derived from sources you are not allergic to.

15.2: Safe Herbal Options for Children

Chamomile and Fennel Tummy Tea

Beneficial effects

Chamomile and Fennel Tummy Tea is a gentle, soothing remedy designed for children experiencing digestive discomfort, such as bloating, gas, and stomach cramps. Chamomile is renowned for its calming and anti-inflammatory properties, which can help relax the muscles of the digestive tract and ease discomfort. Fennel seeds are traditionally used to treat digestive ailments, as they are known to aid in digestion, relieve gas, and reduce bloating. Together, these herbs create a comforting, effective tea that can help soothe a child's upset stomach naturally.

Portions

Makes 2 servings

Preparation time

5 minutes

Cooking time

10 minutes

Ingredients

- 1 tablespoon dried chamomile flowers

- 1 teaspoon fennel seeds

- 2 cups water

- Honey (optional, to taste)

Instructions

1. Begin by bringing 2 cups of water to a boil in a small saucepan.
2. While the water is heating, lightly crush the fennel seeds using a mortar and pestle to release their oils and enhance the tea's flavor and digestive benefits.
3. Once the water reaches a rolling boil, add the crushed fennel seeds and dried chamomile flowers to the saucepan.
4. Cover the saucepan with a lid, reduce the heat, and simmer for 5 minutes. This allows the herbs to infuse the water fully, creating a potent herbal tea.
5. After simmering, remove the saucepan from the heat and let it steep, covered, for an additional 5 minutes. Steeping further enhances the tea's medicinal properties.
6. Strain the tea through a fine mesh strainer into two cups, ensuring that the chamomile flowers and fennel seeds are completely removed.
7. If desired, add a teaspoon of honey to each cup to sweeten the tea. Honey not only improves the taste for children but also offers additional soothing properties for the throat and digestive system.
8. Serve the tea warm, ensuring it's at a comfortable temperature for a child to drink safely.

Variations

- For children who prefer a cooler beverage, allow the tea to cool completely and serve it over ice for a refreshing, stomach-soothing drink.

- Add a slice of ginger while simmering the tea to provide additional digestive benefits and a warming flavor.

- Mix in a teaspoon of peppermint leaves during the last minute of simmering for a minty flavor and enhanced digestive soothing effects.

Storage tips

Store any leftover tea in the refrigerator in a sealed glass container for up to 24 hours. Gently reheat the tea when ready to serve again, or serve it cold, depending on preference.

Tips for allergens

For children with sensitivities to honey, consider using maple syrup as a natural, gentle sweetener alternative. Always ensure that the child has no allergies to chamomile, fennel, or any other ingredients used in the tea before serving.

Lemon Balm and Honey Sleep Aid

Beneficial effects

Lemon Balm and Honey Sleep Aid harnesses the calming properties of lemon balm and the soothing effects of honey to promote relaxation and sleep. Lemon balm, a member of the mint family, has been used for centuries to reduce stress, anxiety, and improve sleep quality due to its mild sedative properties. Honey, rich in antioxidants, can provide a comforting effect and when consumed before bed, may contribute to the release of melatonin in the brain, enhancing sleep quality. This gentle, natural remedy is suitable for children, offering a safe and effective way to help them relax and drift off to sleep.

Portions

Makes approximately 2 servings

Preparation time

5 minutes

Cooking time

10 minutes

Ingredients

- 2 cups of water

- 2 tablespoons dried lemon balm leaves

- 2 teaspoons honey, or to taste

Instructions

1. Bring 2 cups of water to a boil in a small saucepan.
2. Once the water is boiling, remove the saucepan from the heat.
3. Add 2 tablespoons of dried lemon balm leaves to the hot water. If using a tea infuser or tea bag, place the leaves inside before adding them to the water.
4. Cover the saucepan with a lid and allow the lemon balm to steep for 8-10 minutes. The longer it steeps, the stronger the flavor and calming effects will be.
5. After steeping, strain the lemon balm leaves from the water using a fine mesh strainer or remove the tea infuser or tea bag.
6. Stir 2 teaspoons of honey into the warm lemon balm tea until fully dissolved. Adjust the amount of honey according to taste preference.
7. Serve the Lemon Balm and Honey Sleep Aid warm, ideally 30 minutes before bedtime to help prepare for sleep.

Variations

- For additional flavor and sleep-promoting benefits, add a cinnamon stick or a few slices of fresh ginger to the water before boiling.

- Incorporate a teaspoon of chamomile flowers along with lemon balm for an even more potent sleep aid.

- If preparing for adults or older children, a slice of lemon can be added for a refreshing twist and a dose of vitamin C.

Storage tips

The Lemon Balm and Honey Sleep Aid is best enjoyed fresh. However, if necessary, it can be stored in the refrigerator for up to 24 hours. Reheat gently on the stove or in the microwave before serving. Store dried lemon balm leaves in an airtight container in a cool, dark place to maintain their potency.

Tips for allergens

Individuals with allergies to plants in the mint family should proceed with caution when using lemon balm. Honey should not be given to children under 1 year of age due to the risk of botulism. For those with honey allergies or sensitivities, maple syrup can be used as a substitute, though it may alter the flavor profile.

Marshmallow Root Soothing Syrup

Beneficial effects

Marshmallow Root Soothing Syrup is a gentle, natural remedy designed to alleviate coughs and sore throats in children. The mucilaginous properties of marshmallow root form a protective layer on the throat's lining, soothing irritation and reducing inflammation. This makes it an excellent choice for treating dry coughs and providing relief from the discomfort associated with minor throat infections.

Portions

Makes approximately 8 ounces

Preparation time

10 minutes

Cooking time

20 minutes

Ingredients

- 1/4 cup dried marshmallow root

- 1 cup water

- 1 cup honey, preferably local and organic

Instructions

1. Combine 1/4 cup of dried marshmallow root with 1 cup of water in a small saucepan.
2. Bring the mixture to a boil, then reduce the heat and simmer for 20 minutes. This slow cooking process allows the water to become infused with the marshmallow root's beneficial properties.

3. After simmering, strain the liquid through a fine mesh strainer or cheesecloth into a heat-resistant bowl, pressing or squeezing the marshmallow root to extract as much liquid as possible. Discard the used marshmallow root.
4. While the liquid is still warm (but not hot), add 1 cup of honey to the marshmallow root infusion. Stir thoroughly until the honey is completely dissolved. The warmth of the liquid will help to integrate the honey smoothly.
5. Pour the finished syrup into a clean, dry bottle or jar with a tight-fitting lid.

Variations

- For added flavor and immune support, stir in 1 teaspoon of cinnamon or ginger powder to the syrup while mixing in the honey.

- If the syrup is too thick, adjust the consistency by adding a little more water until the desired thickness is achieved.

Storage tips

Store the Marshmallow Root Soothing Syrup in the refrigerator for up to 2 months. Ensure the container is sealed tightly to maintain freshness and prevent contamination.

Tips for allergens

For children with honey allergies or those under 1 year of age (due to the risk of botulism with honey), substitute the honey with maple syrup or glycerin to maintain the syrup's soothing properties without using honey.

Chapter 16: Digestive Health

16.1: Managing Digestive Upset

Ginger Mint Digestive Aid

Beneficial effects

Ginger Mint Digestive Aid is designed to soothe digestive discomfort, such as bloating, gas, and indigestion. Ginger, with its natural anti-inflammatory and gastrointestinal motility properties, helps to relieve nausea and speed up the emptying of the stomach. Mint, specifically peppermint, has been shown to relax the digestive system and ease pain. Together, they create a powerful duo that can help alleviate common digestive issues, making this tea an excellent choice for those seeking natural remedies for digestive health.

Portions

Makes 2 servings

Preparation time

5 minutes

Cooking time

10 minutes

Ingredients

- 1 tablespoon fresh ginger root, thinly sliced

- 1 tablespoon fresh mint leaves, or 1 teaspoon dried mint

- 2 cups water

- Honey or lemon (optional, to taste)

Instructions

1. Begin by washing the fresh ginger root and mint leaves under cold running water. Pat them dry with a clean towel.
2. Thinly slice the ginger root to maximize the surface area for infusion. If using fresh mint leaves, gently bruise them with the back of a spoon to release their essential oils.
3. In a small saucepan, bring 2 cups of water to a boil. Once boiling, add the sliced ginger and mint leaves to the water.
4. Reduce the heat to low and let the mixture simmer for about 10 minutes. This allows the ginger and mint to infuse the water, creating a potent digestive aid.
5. After simmering, remove the saucepan from the heat. Strain the tea through a fine mesh strainer into teacups or mugs, discarding the ginger slices and mint leaves.
6. If desired, add honey or a squeeze of lemon to each cup for additional flavor and digestive benefits. Honey can provide a soothing sweetness, while lemon adds a refreshing tang and vitamin C.
7. Stir well to ensure any added honey or lemon is fully dissolved, then serve the tea warm for the best soothing effects.

Variations

- For a stronger mint flavor, add more fresh mint leaves or allow the tea to steep for an additional 5 minutes before straining.

- Incorporate a cinnamon stick during the simmering process for added warmth and to further aid in digestion.

- For those preferring a caffeine boost, add a bag of green tea during the last 3 minutes of simmering.

Storage tips

This Ginger Mint Digestive Aid is best enjoyed fresh. However, if you have leftovers or wish to prepare in advance, store the cooled tea in a sealed glass container in the refrigerator for up to 24 hours. Gently reheat on the stove or enjoy chilled.

Tips for allergens

For individuals with allergies to honey, substitute it with maple syrup for a similar sweetness without the allergen. Ensure that all ingredients, especially if substituting dried herbs for fresh, are free from cross-contaminants that could trigger allergies.

Fennel and Chamomile Soothing Tea

Beneficial effects

Fennel and Chamomile Soothing Tea is a natural remedy designed to ease digestive upset, including bloating, gas, and discomfort. Fennel seeds are known for their antispasmodic and gas-relieving properties, helping to relax the digestive tract and alleviate symptoms of indigestion. Chamomile, on the other hand, is celebrated for its anti-inflammatory and calming effects, which can soothe the stomach lining and reduce digestive discomfort. Together, these herbs create a gentle, effective tea that supports digestive health and promotes relaxation.

Portions

Makes 2 servings

Preparation time

5 minutes

Cooking time

10 minutes

Ingredients

- 1 tablespoon dried chamomile flowers

- 1 teaspoon fennel seeds

- 2 cups boiling water

- Honey or lemon to taste (optional)

Instructions

1. Place the fennel seeds in a dry pan over medium heat. Toast them lightly for 1-2 minutes until they become aromatic. This step helps to release the essential oils in the fennel seeds, enhancing their digestive benefits.
2. In a teapot or heat-resistant pitcher, combine the toasted fennel seeds and dried chamomile flowers.
3. Pour 2 cups of boiling water over the chamomile and fennel. Cover the teapot or pitcher with a lid or a plate to keep the steam in, which aids in the infusion process.

4. Allow the tea to steep for 8-10 minutes. Steeping for this duration ensures that the medicinal qualities of both the chamomile and fennel are well extracted into the water.

5. Strain the tea through a fine mesh sieve into two cups, pressing against the chamomile flowers and fennel seeds with a spoon to extract as much liquid and beneficial properties as possible.

6. If desired, sweeten each cup with honey or add a squeeze of lemon for flavor. Honey can provide additional soothing properties for the throat, while lemon adds a refreshing tang and can aid in digestion.

Variations

- For an extra soothing effect, add a slice of fresh ginger to the tea while it steeps. Ginger has anti-inflammatory properties and can further aid in digestion.

- Incorporate a pinch of peppermint leaves to the blend for a refreshing taste and additional digestive benefits.

- To make a cold soothing tea, allow the tea to cool completely, then refrigerate. Serve over ice for a refreshing digestive aid during warmer months.

Storage tips

The tea is best enjoyed fresh, but any leftovers can be stored in the refrigerator for up to 24 hours. Reheat gently or enjoy cold.

Tips for allergens

For those with sensitivities to honey, a simple alternative is to sweeten the tea with maple syrup or to enjoy it unsweetened. Ensure that individuals with pollen allergies are aware of the chamomile content, as chamomile is related to ragweed and may trigger allergies in susceptible individuals.

Caraway Seed Stomach Soother

Beneficial effects

Caraway Seed Stomach Soother offers natural relief for digestive issues such as bloating, gas, and mild spasms. Caraway seeds contain carvone and limonene, compounds that can help relax digestive tract muscles and promote the expulsion of gas, reducing discomfort. This remedy harnesses the antispasmodic and carminative properties of caraway, making it an effective, gentle solution for acute digestive upset.

Portions

Makes about 2 cups

Preparation time

5 minutes

Cooking time

10 minutes

Ingredients

- 2 tablespoons caraway seeds

- 2 cups boiling water

- Optional: Honey or lemon to taste

Instructions

1. Place the caraway seeds in a dry pan over medium heat. Toast them lightly for 1-2 minutes, stirring constantly to prevent burning. Toasting the seeds helps release their essential oils, enhancing the tea's effectiveness and flavor.
2. Boil 2 cups of water in a kettle or saucepan.
3. Once the water reaches a rolling boil, remove it from the heat.
4. Add the toasted caraway seeds to the boiling water. If using a tea infuser or mesh tea ball, place the seeds inside before submerging in water.
5. Cover and steep the caraway seeds in hot water for 8-10 minutes. The longer steeping time allows for a stronger infusion, maximizing the digestive benefits.
6. Strain the caraway seeds from the water using a fine mesh strainer, or remove the tea infuser or mesh tea ball.
7. If desired, add honey or a squeeze of lemon to the tea for flavor. Honey can provide a soothing sweetness, while lemon adds a refreshing tang and may enhance the digestive benefits.
8. Serve the tea warm for immediate relief from digestive discomfort.

Variations

- For additional digestive support, consider adding a teaspoon of crushed fennel seeds to the infusion along with the caraway seeds. Fennel further aids in reducing gas and bloating.

- Incorporate a slice of fresh ginger during the steeping process for its anti-inflammatory and gastrointestinal soothing properties.

- To create a cooling, refreshing beverage for warm weather or to soothe an upset stomach, allow the tea to cool completely and serve it over ice.

Storage tips

Store any leftover Caraway Seed Stomach Soother in a sealed glass container in the refrigerator for up to 2 days. Reheat gently on the stove or enjoy cold, depending on personal preference.

Tips for allergens

For those with honey allergies or sensitivities, substitute honey with maple syrup for sweetness without compromising the soothing properties of the tea. Ensure any additional herbs or spices used are compatible with individual dietary restrictions or allergies.

16.2: Supporting Long-Term Digestive Wellness

Probiotic Yogurt Smoothie

Beneficial effects

Probiotic Yogurt Smoothie is a nourishing beverage that supports long-term digestive wellness by incorporating the health benefits of probiotics found in yogurt. Probiotics are live bacteria and yeasts that are good for your digestive system, helping to balance the gut microbiome, enhance immune function, and reduce symptoms of digestive disorders. This smoothie also provides a healthy dose of calcium, protein, and essential vitamins, making it an excellent choice for a nutrient-rich start to the day or a rejuvenating midday snack.

Portions

Makes 2 servings

Preparation time

5 minutes

Cooking time

No cooking required

Ingredients

- 1 cup plain, unsweetened probiotic yogurt
- 1/2 cup fresh or frozen blueberries
- 1/2 banana, sliced
- 1 tablespoon honey or maple syrup (optional)
- 1/2 cup ice cubes
- 1/4 cup water or almond milk, for desired consistency

Instructions

1. In a blender, combine 1 cup of plain, unsweetened probiotic yogurt with 1/2 cup of fresh or frozen blueberries and 1/2 of a sliced banana.
2. Add 1 tablespoon of honey or maple syrup to the blender for a touch of sweetness, if desired. This step is optional and can be adjusted based on personal taste preferences.
3. Add 1/2 cup of ice cubes to the mixture to create a chilled, refreshing smoothie.
4. Pour 1/4 cup of water or almond milk into the blender. Start with a smaller amount and gradually add more to achieve the desired consistency of the smoothie.
5. Blend the ingredients on high speed until smooth and creamy, ensuring there are no large chunks of fruit or ice remaining.
6. Taste the smoothie and adjust the sweetness or consistency if necessary, by adding a little more honey or liquid, then blend again briefly.
7. Once the smoothie reaches your preferred taste and texture, pour it into two glasses and serve immediately for the freshest flavor and maximum probiotic benefits.

Variations

- For an added nutritional boost, include a handful of spinach or kale to the smoothie before blending. These greens will increase the fiber content without significantly altering the taste.

- Substitute blueberries with other antioxidant-rich fruits like strawberries, raspberries, or mango for different flavor profiles and nutritional benefits.

- Add a tablespoon of chia seeds or flaxseeds to the smoothie for extra fiber and omega-3 fatty acids, which can further support digestive health.

Storage tips

This Probiotic Yogurt Smoothie is best enjoyed immediately after blending to take advantage of the live probiotics and fresh flavors. However, if needed, it can be stored in a sealed container in the refrigerator for up to 24 hours. Stir well before serving if separation occurs.

Tips for allergens

For those with dairy sensitivities or lactose intolerance, substitute the probiotic yogurt with a dairy-free alternative such as coconut yogurt or almond milk yogurt that contains live probiotic cultures. Ensure the substitute is unsweetened to control the sugar content of the smoothie.

Fermented Carrot Sticks

Beneficial effects

Fermented Carrot Sticks are a rich source of probiotics, essential for maintaining a healthy gut microbiome. The fermentation process enhances the bioavailability of nutrients in carrots, making them easier to digest while providing beneficial bacteria that support gut health. Regular consumption can aid in improving digestion, boosting the immune system, and may help in preventing gastrointestinal issues.

Portions

Makes approximately 1 quart

Preparation time

15 minutes (plus 3-5 days for fermentation)

Cooking time

No cooking required

Ingredients

- 1 pound organic carrots, peeled and cut into sticks

- 3 cloves of garlic, peeled and lightly crushed

- 2 tablespoons sea salt

- 4 cups filtered water

- 1 teaspoon dill seeds or fresh dill (optional)

- 2 bay leaves

- 1/2 teaspoon black peppercorn

Instructions

1. Dissolve 2 tablespoons of sea salt in 4 cups of filtered water to create a brine. Ensure the salt is completely dissolved.
2. Sterilize a 1-quart glass jar by boiling it in water for 10 minutes. Allow it to cool before use.
3. Place the lightly crushed garlic cloves, dill seeds (if using), bay leaves, and black peppercorns at the bottom of the jar.
4. Tightly pack the carrot sticks vertically into the jar, leaving about an inch of space from the top.

5. Pour the saltwater brine over the carrots, ensuring they are completely submerged. Leave about 1/2 inch of space at the top. If necessary, place a small fermentation weight or a clean, boiled rock on top of the carrots to keep them submerged.
6. Seal the jar with its lid, but not too tightly. Gas produced during fermentation needs to escape.
7. Store the jar at room temperature, away from direct sunlight, for 3-5 days. Check daily to ensure carrots remain submerged, pressing them down if they have floated to the top.
8. Begin tasting the carrots after 3 days. Once they've reached your desired level of tanginess, tighten the jar's lid and refrigerate. Fermentation will slow down but continue at a much slower pace in the refrigerator.

Variations

- For a spicier kick, add a sliced jalapeño or a few dashes of red pepper flakes to the jar before adding the carrots.

- Incorporate a few slices of ginger for an additional flavor dimension and digestive benefits.

- Replace dill with other herbs like thyme or rosemary for a different flavor profile.

Storage tips

Store the fermented carrot sticks in the refrigerator for up to 2 months. Ensure the carrots remain submerged in the brine to prevent mold growth.

Tips for allergens

For those with garlic or dill sensitivities, simply omit these ingredients from the recipe. The fermentation process will still occur, producing flavorful and probiotic-rich carrot sticks.

Herbal Digestive Bitters

Beneficial effects

Herbal Digestive Bitters are designed to stimulate the digestive system, promoting the production of digestive enzymes, bile, and stomach acid, which are essential for breaking down food and absorbing nutrients effectively. By enhancing natural digestion, these bitters can help alleviate common digestive issues such as bloating, gas, and indigestion. Their use supports long-term digestive wellness by encouraging the body's innate digestive processes, making them a valuable addition to a holistic approach to health.

Portions

Makes about 16 ounces

Preparation time

15 minutes (plus 2-4 weeks for infusing)

Cooking time

No cooking required

Ingredients

- 1/2 cup dried dandelion root

- 1/2 cup dried gentian root

- 1/4 cup dried orange peel

- 1/4 cup dried fennel seeds

- 2 tablespoons dried ginger root

- 1 tablespoon dried peppermint leaves

- 16 ounces of 100-proof vodka or apple cider vinegar (for a non-alcoholic version)

Instructions

1. Combine dried dandelion root, gentian root, orange peel, fennel seeds, ginger root, and peppermint leaves in a clean, dry quart-sized jar.
2. Pour 16 ounces of 100-proof vodka or apple cider vinegar over the herbs, ensuring they are completely submerged. If using vinegar, ensure it covers the herbs by at least two inches, as it does not extract as efficiently as alcohol.
3. Seal the jar tightly with a lid. Shake gently to mix the contents.
4. Label the jar with the date and contents. Store in a cool, dark place for 2-4 weeks, shaking the jar every few days to aid in the extraction process.
5. After the infusion period, strain the mixture through a fine mesh strainer or cheesecloth into a clean bottle, pressing or squeezing the herbs to extract as much liquid as possible. Discard the herbs.
6. Transfer the strained liquid into dark glass dropper bottles for easy use.

Variations

- For added flavor complexity and digestive benefits, include a teaspoon of cardamom pods or a cinnamon stick to the herb mixture before infusing.

- To sweeten the bitters and enhance their palatability, dissolve a tablespoon of honey into the strained liquid before bottling. Ensure the liquid is at room temperature to effectively mix in the honey.

Storage tips

Store the Herbal Digestive Bitters in a cool, dark place. The alcohol version will last indefinitely, while the vinegar-based bitters should be consumed within 6 months for optimal potency.

Tips for allergens

For those with allergies to specific herbs, substitute or omit the offending herbs from the recipe. Always consult with a healthcare provider before starting any new herbal regimen, especially if you have existing health conditions or are taking medications.

Chapter 17: Energy and Vitality

17.1: Herbs to Combat Fatigue

Ginseng Energy Elixir

Beneficial effects

Ginseng Energy Elixir harnesses the revitalizing power of ginseng, renowned for its ability to boost energy levels, improve mental clarity, and combat fatigue. This ancient herb has been used for thousands of years in traditional medicine to enhance physical and mental endurance. Its adaptogenic properties help the body to better manage stress, making it an ideal tonic for those looking to increase their vitality and resilience to daily pressures.

Portions

Makes about 2 cups

Preparation time

15 minutes

Cooking time

No cooking required

Ingredients

- 4 tablespoons of dried ginseng root

- 2 cups of filtered water

- 2 tablespoons of raw honey

- Juice of 1 lemon

- A pinch of ground cinnamon (optional)

Instructions

1. Begin by finely chopping or grinding the dried ginseng root to increase the surface area for extraction.
2. Place the ginseng in a glass jar and pour 2 cups of filtered water over it. Ensure the water is at room temperature to preserve the herb's beneficial properties.
3. Seal the jar tightly and let it sit at room temperature for 24 hours, allowing the ginseng to infuse into the water.
4. After 24 hours, strain the mixture through a fine mesh strainer or cheesecloth into a new jar, squeezing or pressing the ginseng to extract as much liquid as possible. Discard the ginseng solids.
5. Stir in 2 tablespoons of raw honey to the ginseng infusion until fully dissolved. The honey not only adds sweetness but also enhances the tonic's energy-boosting effects.
6. Add the juice of 1 lemon to the mixture, providing a refreshing taste and vitamin C, which aids in the absorption of the ginseng's active compounds.
7. If desired, add a pinch of ground cinnamon for additional flavor and its blood sugar-regulating benefits.
8. Mix well to ensure all ingredients are thoroughly combined.
9. Pour the elixir into a clean bottle and refrigerate until ready to use.

Variations

- For an extra energy boost, add a teaspoon of matcha powder to the elixir, mixing well to combine. Matcha contains caffeine and is rich in antioxidants.

- Incorporate a slice of fresh ginger during the infusion process for its warming effects and to aid digestion.

- Replace honey with maple syrup for a vegan-friendly version of the elixir.

Storage tips

Store the Ginseng Energy Elixir in the refrigerator for up to 1 week. Shake well before each use as natural separation may occur.

Tips for allergens

Individuals with allergies to honey can substitute it with agave syrup or another sweetener of choice. For those sensitive to ginseng, start with a smaller amount to assess tolerance.

Ashwagandha Vitality Tonic

Beneficial effects

Ashwagandha Vitality Tonic is crafted to combat fatigue and enhance energy levels naturally. Ashwagandha, known for its adaptogenic properties, helps the body manage stress and improves stamina. This tonic supports adrenal function, boosts energy without the crash associated with caffeine, and promotes overall vitality and well-being.

Portions

Makes about 2 cups

Preparation time

5 minutes

Cooking time

No cooking required

Ingredients

- 2 cups of filtered water
- 1 tablespoon ashwagandha powder
- 1 teaspoon raw honey (optional, for sweetness)
- 1/2 teaspoon cinnamon powder (for flavor and blood sugar regulation)
- A pinch of ground cardamom (for digestive support)
- A pinch of ground ginger (for added energy and digestion aid)

Instructions

1. Start by measuring 2 cups of filtered water into a large glass jar or bottle.
2. Add 1 tablespoon of ashwagandha powder to the water. Secure the lid on the jar and shake vigorously to ensure the ashwagandha is fully dissolved.
3. Once the ashwagandha is mixed in, open the jar and add 1 teaspoon of raw honey, 1/2 teaspoon of cinnamon powder, a pinch of ground cardamom, and a pinch of ground ginger to the mixture.
4. Secure the lid back on the jar and shake again until all the ingredients are well combined and the honey is dissolved.
5. Taste the tonic and adjust the sweetness or spices according to your preference by adding more honey or spices and shaking well after each addition.
6. For best results, let the tonic sit for about an hour in the refrigerator to allow the flavors to meld together and the ashwagandha to fully infuse into the water.
7. Serve the tonic chilled. Shake well before each use as the ashwagandha may settle at the bottom.

Variations

- For a refreshing twist, add a few slices of fresh lemon or orange to the tonic. The citrus will add a vibrant flavor and vitamin C.

- Incorporate a tablespoon of fresh grated ginger instead of ground ginger for a more potent digestive aid and energy boost.

- If you prefer a creamier texture, blend the tonic with a tablespoon of almond butter for added richness and a boost of healthy fats.

Storage tips

Store the Ashwagandha Vitality Tonic in a sealed glass container in the refrigerator for up to 5 days. Shake well before each use to redistribute any settled ashwagandha powder.

Tips for allergens

For those with honey allergies or vegan preferences, substitute honey with maple syrup or agave nectar to maintain the natural sweetness without using animal products. Ensure all spices used are pure and free from cross-contamination with allergens.

Rhodiola Rosea Revitalizing Tea

Beneficial effects

Rhodiola Rosea Revitalizing Tea is designed to combat fatigue and enhance energy levels naturally. Rhodiola Rosea, often referred to as the "golden root," is an adaptogen that helps the body adapt to and resist physical, chemical, and environmental stress. By improving your body's stress response, this herbal tea can increase stamina, reduce exhaustion, and promote mental clarity and concentration. Regular consumption may lead to improved endurance during physical activities, enhanced mental performance, and a balanced mood.

Portions

Makes 2 servings

Preparation time

5 minutes

Cooking time

10 minutes

Ingredients

- 2 teaspoons dried Rhodiola Rosea root
- 2 cups water
- Honey or lemon to taste (optional)
- A pinch of cinnamon or ginger (optional, for flavor)

Instructions

1. Bring 2 cups of water to a boil in a small saucepan.
2. Add 2 teaspoons of dried Rhodiola Rosea root to the boiling water. If you have a tea infuser or mesh tea ball, use it to contain the roots for easy removal.
3. Reduce the heat to low and let the tea simmer for 10 minutes. This slow simmering process allows the water to become infused with the adaptogenic properties of Rhodiola Rosea.
4. After simmering, remove the saucepan from the heat. If you did not use a tea infuser, strain the tea through a fine mesh strainer to remove the Rhodiola Rosea roots.
5. If desired, add honey or a squeeze of lemon to the tea for flavor. A pinch of cinnamon or ginger can also be added for an extra warming and stimulating taste.
6. Stir well to ensure any added ingredients are fully dissolved, then serve the tea warm.

Variations

- For a refreshing twist, allow the tea to cool and serve it over ice. This makes for a revitalizing cold drink, especially beneficial during warmer months or after physical activities.

- Blend the tea with a small amount of fresh orange juice for a citrusy flavor and added vitamin C, which can further support the immune system.

- Incorporate a teaspoon of ashwagandha powder to the tea to enhance its adaptogenic effects and further support stress relief and energy levels.

Storage tips

Rhodiola Rosea Revitalizing Tea is best enjoyed fresh. However, if you need to store it, keep the tea in a sealed glass container in the refrigerator for up to 24 hours. Reheat gently on the stove or enjoy cold, depending on your preference.

Tips for allergens

For those with sensitivities to honey, substitute it with maple syrup or simply enjoy the tea without sweeteners to maintain its natural flavor profile. Ensure that any additional herbs or spices used are compatible with your dietary restrictions or allergies.

17.2: Adaptogens for Long-Term Resilience

Ashwagandha Stress Relief Elixir

Beneficial effects

Ashwagandha Stress Relief Elixir utilizes the adaptogenic properties of ashwagandha to help the body manage stress, reduce anxiety, and support overall well-being. Adaptogens like ashwagandha are known for their ability to balance cortisol levels, which can help mitigate the effects of stress on the body. Regular intake of this elixir can lead to improved energy levels, enhanced mood, and a more resilient stress response, making it a valuable addition to a daily wellness routine.

Portions

Makes about 2 cups

Preparation time

10 minutes

Ingredients

- 2 cups filtered water

- 1 tablespoon ashwagandha powder

- 1 teaspoon honey (optional, for sweetness)

- 1/4 teaspoon ground cinnamon (for flavor and to aid in balancing blood sugar levels)

- A pinch of ground ginger (to enhance absorption and add a warming effect)

- A pinch of ground cardamom (for digestive support and added flavor)

Instructions

1. Pour 2 cups of filtered water into a medium-sized saucepan and bring to a low simmer over medium heat.
2. Reduce the heat to low and whisk in 1 tablespoon of ashwagandha powder until fully dissolved in the water.
3. Add a pinch of ground ginger and a pinch of ground cardamom to the mixture, stirring continuously to ensure the spices are well integrated.

4. Simmer the mixture on low heat for 5 minutes, allowing the flavors to meld together and the ashwagandha to infuse into the water.
5. Remove the saucepan from the heat and let it cool for a few minutes.
6. Stir in 1 teaspoon of honey and 1/4 teaspoon of ground cinnamon to the warm mixture, adjusting the amount of honey to taste.
7. Once the honey and cinnamon are fully incorporated, strain the elixir through a fine mesh strainer into a glass or mug to remove any undissolved particles.
8. Serve the Ashwagandha Stress Relief Elixir warm, or allow it to cool and enjoy it at room temperature depending on your preference.

Variations

- For a cold, refreshing version, let the elixir cool completely and then refrigerate for 1-2 hours. Serve over ice with a slice of lemon for an added antioxidant boost.

- Blend the cooled elixir with a handful of fresh mint leaves and a squeeze of lime juice for a refreshing herbal twist.

- For those who prefer a creamier texture, mix the cooled elixir with almond milk or coconut milk instead of water for a latte-like beverage.

Storage tips

Store any leftover Ashwagandha Stress Relief Elixir in a sealed glass container in the refrigerator for up to 48 hours. Gently shake or stir before serving, as natural separation may occur.

Tips for allergens

For individuals with honey allergies or those following a vegan diet, substitute honey with maple syrup or agave nectar to maintain the natural sweetness without using animal products. Ensure that the ashwagandha powder used is certified organic and free from cross-contaminants to avoid potential allergens.

Eleuthero Root Resilience Tonic

Beneficial effects

Eleuthero Root Resilience Tonic is designed to enhance physical and mental resilience, helping the body adapt to stress more effectively. Eleuthero, also known as Siberian Ginseng, is a powerful adaptogen that increases stamina, reduces fatigue, and improves overall energy levels. Regular consumption can support the immune system, enhance cognitive function, and help the body maintain balance during stressful periods. This tonic is particularly beneficial for those seeking natural ways to sustain energy and focus without the side effects of stimulants.

Portions

Makes about 2 cups

Preparation time

10 minutes

Cooking time

No cooking required

Ingredients

- 2 tablespoons dried Eleuthero root

- 2 cups of cold water

- 1 tablespoon honey, or to taste

- Juice of 1/2 lemon

- A pinch of ground cinnamon (optional for additional flavor and blood sugar support)

Instructions

1. Place 2 tablespoons of dried Eleuthero root into a large glass jar or pitcher.
2. Pour 2 cups of cold water over the Eleuthero root, ensuring the roots are fully submerged.
3. Seal the jar or pitcher with a lid or cover and refrigerate overnight, allowing the Eleuthero root to infuse into the water.
4. The next day, strain the infusion through a fine mesh sieve into another jar or pitcher, pressing on the Eleuthero root to extract as much liquid as possible. Discard the roots.
5. Stir in 1 tablespoon of honey into the Eleuthero infusion until fully dissolved, adjusting the amount according to your sweetness preference.
6. Add the juice of 1/2 lemon to the tonic, mixing well to incorporate.
7. For additional flavor and health benefits, sprinkle a pinch of ground cinnamon into the tonic and stir thoroughly.
8. Serve the tonic chilled. For best results, consume in the morning to kickstart your day or in the early afternoon to avoid a midday energy slump.

Variations

- For a refreshing twist, add a few slices of fresh ginger or a sprig of mint to the infusion for a zesty or cooling flavor.

- Replace honey with maple syrup for a vegan-friendly sweetener option.

- Incorporate a splash of apple cider vinegar for added digestive benefits and a tangy taste.

Storage tips

Keep the Eleuthero Root Resilience Tonic refrigerated and consume within 5 days for optimal freshness and efficacy. Store in a glass container to preserve the flavors and benefits of the ingredients..

Book 5: The Apothecary Shelf – Recipes and Solutions

Chapter 18: Ailment-by-Ailment Reference Guide

18.1: Natural Pain Relief Recipes

Turmeric and Ginger Muscle Rub

Beneficial effects

Turmeric and Ginger Muscle Rub combines the anti-inflammatory and analgesic properties of turmeric with the warming and soothing effects of ginger, creating a natural remedy for relieving muscle pain and stiffness. Turmeric contains curcumin, a compound known for its ability to reduce inflammation and pain, while ginger improves circulation and alleviates discomfort. This rub is ideal for those seeking a natural approach to manage muscle soreness and enhance recovery after physical activity.

Ingredients

- 1/4 cup coconut oil

- 2 tablespoons grated beeswax

- 1 tablespoon turmeric powder

- 1 tablespoon ginger powder

- 10 drops peppermint essential oil

- 10 drops lavender essential oil

Instructions

1. Begin by setting up a double boiler: fill a pot with a few inches of water and place it on the stove over medium heat. Place a heat-safe bowl on top of the pot, ensuring the bottom of the bowl does not touch the water.
2. Add 1/4 cup coconut oil and 2 tablespoons grated beeswax to the bowl. Stir occasionally as the mixture melts, combining the ingredients thoroughly.
3. Once the coconut oil and beeswax are fully melted and mixed, reduce the heat to low. Carefully stir in 1 tablespoon turmeric powder and 1 tablespoon ginger powder until completely incorporated into the mixture.
4. Remove the bowl from the heat. Allow the mixture to cool slightly for a few minutes, but not solidify.
5. Stir in 10 drops of peppermint essential oil and 10 drops of lavender essential oil into the slightly cooled mixture. These oils add additional pain-relieving properties and a soothing fragrance.

6. Pour the mixture into a clean, dry container, such as a small glass jar or metal tin. Let it sit uncovered until it solidifies completely.

7. Once solidified, cover the container with a lid to preserve the rub's potency and aroma.

Variations

- For extra heat, add a teaspoon of cayenne pepper powder to the mixture. Cayenne pepper is known for its capsaicin content, which can help reduce pain.

- Substitute coconut oil with shea butter for a thicker consistency and additional moisturizing benefits.

- For a vegan option, use candelilla wax instead of beeswax, adjusting the quantity as needed to achieve the desired consistency.

Storage tips

Store the Turmeric and Ginger Muscle Rub in a cool, dry place away from direct sunlight. If stored properly, the rub can last for up to 6 months. The consistency may change in extreme temperatures, so keep it at a stable room temperature to maintain its form.

Tips for allergens

Individuals with sensitivities to any of the essential oils can omit them or substitute with oils that are better tolerated, such as eucalyptus or chamomile essential oil, which also have soothing properties. Always perform a patch test on a small area of skin before applying the rub extensively, especially if you have sensitive skin or allergies to any ingredients.

Peppermint and Lavender Headache Balm

Beneficial effects

Peppermint and Lavender Headache Balm combines the natural analgesic properties of peppermint oil, which can relieve headache pain through a cooling effect and increased blood flow, with the calming and anti-inflammatory benefits of lavender oil, known to reduce stress and tension that can contribute to headaches. This balm offers a natural, therapeutic alternative to over-the-counter headache remedies, providing relief through a holistic approach that engages the body's own healing mechanisms.

Portions

Makes about 2 ounces

Preparation time

10 minutes

Cooking time

5 minutes

Ingredients

- 2 tablespoons coconut oil

- 2 tablespoons shea butter

- 1 tablespoon beeswax pellets

- 10 drops peppermint essential oil

- 10 drops lavender essential oil

- Small glass jar or metal tin for storage

Instructions

1. Begin by setting up a double boiler: fill a pot with a couple of inches of water and place it on the stove over medium heat. Place a heat-safe glass bowl on top of the pot, ensuring the bottom of the bowl does not touch the water.
2. Add 2 tablespoons of coconut oil, 2 tablespoons of shea butter, and 1 tablespoon of beeswax pellets to the glass bowl. Stir occasionally as the mixture melts, combining the ingredients into a smooth, uniform liquid.
3. Once fully melted and combined, carefully remove the bowl from the heat. Allow the mixture to cool for a minute or two, but not solidify.
4. Stir in 10 drops of peppermint essential oil and 10 drops of lavender essential oil into the slightly cooled mixture. Mix thoroughly to ensure the essential oils are well distributed throughout the balm.
5. Carefully pour the liquid balm into a small glass jar or metal tin. Allow the balm to cool and solidify at room temperature. This process may take a couple of hours.
6. Once solidified, secure the lid on the container to keep the balm protected and prevent it from melting.

Variations

- For a vegan version, substitute beeswax pellets with candelilla wax, using half the amount as it's denser than beeswax.

- Add a few drops of eucalyptus oil for an extra sinus-clearing effect, especially beneficial for headaches associated with sinus pressure.

- For those sensitive to strong scents, reduce the amount of essential oils by half.

Storage tips

Store the Peppermint and Lavender Headache Balm in a cool, dry place away from direct sunlight. If stored properly, the balm can last for up to a year. In warmer climates or seasons, consider refrigerating the balm to maintain its solid state.

Tips for allergens

For individuals with sensitivities to coconut oil, substitute it with another carrier oil such as almond oil or jojoba oil. Always perform a patch test on a small area of skin before widespread use, especially for those with sensitive skin or allergies to essential oils.

18.2: Natural Remedies for Anxiety and Mood

Lemon Balm Anxiety Relief Tea

Beneficial effects

Lemon Balm Anxiety Relief Tea harnesses the calming properties of lemon balm, a herb known for its ability to alleviate stress, reduce anxiety, and promote a sense of calm. This gentle yet effective herbal remedy can help soothe the nervous system, making it an excellent choice for those seeking natural methods to manage daily stress and improve overall mental well-being.

Portions

Makes 2 servings

Preparation time

5 minutes

Cooking time

10 minutes

Ingredients

- 2 tablespoons dried lemon balm leaves

- 2 cups boiling water

- Honey or lemon to taste (optional)

Instructions

1. Boil 2 cups of water in a kettle or saucepan.
2. Place 2 tablespoons of dried lemon balm leaves in a teapot or a heat-resistant pitcher.
3. Once the water reaches a rolling boil, pour it over the lemon balm leaves in the teapot or pitcher.
4. Cover the teapot or pitcher with a lid or a plate to retain the heat and allow the lemon balm leaves to steep for 10 minutes. This steeping time lets the lemon balm release its essential oils and active compounds into the water, maximizing the tea's calming effects.
5. After steeping, strain the lemon balm leaves from the tea using a fine mesh sieve or remove the infuser if one was used.
6. If desired, add honey or a squeeze of lemon to the tea for flavor. Honey can provide a soothing sweetness, enhancing the calming experience, while lemon adds a refreshing tang and vitamin C.
7. Stir well to ensure any added honey or lemon is fully dissolved, then serve the tea warm for immediate relaxation benefits.

Variations

- For added relaxation and flavor, include a teaspoon of dried lavender flowers to the steeping process. Lavender has complementary calming effects and can enhance the tea's aroma.

- Mix in a slice of fresh ginger during the steeping for a warming effect and additional digestive benefits.

- For a cooler, refreshing version, allow the tea to cool completely and then refrigerate. Serve over ice for a soothing summer drink.

Storage tips

Lemon Balm Anxiety Relief Tea is best enjoyed fresh, but it can be stored in the refrigerator for up to 24 hours. Store in a sealed glass container to maintain its flavors and calming properties. Gently reheat or enjoy cold, as preferred.

Tips for allergens

For those with honey allergies or following a vegan diet, substitute honey with maple syrup or agave nectar to maintain the natural sweetness without using animal products. Ensure that the lemon balm and any additional herbs used are organic and free from cross-contamination with allergens.

Holy Basil Mood Enhancer

Beneficial effects

Holy Basil Mood Enhancer leverages the adaptogenic and anti-stress properties of Holy Basil (Ocimum sanctum), also known as Tulsi, to naturally uplift mood and alleviate symptoms of stress and anxiety. This revered herb has been used in Ayurvedic medicine for centuries to foster clear thoughts, relaxation, and a sense of well-being. Its ability to balance cortisol levels can help mitigate the physical and emotional effects of stress, making it a valuable ally in today's fast-paced world.

Portions

Makes about 2 cups

Preparation time

10 minutes

Ingredients

- 2 cups of water
- 2 tablespoons dried Holy Basil leaves
- 1 teaspoon honey (optional, for sweetness)
- 1/4 teaspoon ground cinnamon (optional, for flavor and added stress-relief benefits)
- A few drops of lemon juice (optional, for a refreshing twist)

Instructions

1. Bring 2 cups of water to a boil in a medium-sized saucepan.
2. Once the water is boiling, add 2 tablespoons of dried Holy Basil leaves to the saucepan.
3. Reduce the heat to low and let the Holy Basil leaves simmer for about 5 minutes. This gentle simmering process allows the water to become infused with the herb's mood-enhancing properties.
4. After simmering, remove the saucepan from the heat and allow it to cool for a few minutes.
5. Strain the Holy Basil leaves from the water using a fine mesh strainer, pressing on the leaves to extract as much liquid and beneficial properties as possible. Discard the leaves.
6. If desired, stir in 1 teaspoon of honey, a 1/4 teaspoon of ground cinnamon, and a few drops of lemon juice to the Holy Basil infusion. Adjust the sweetness and flavorings according to your preference.
7. Serve the Holy Basil Mood Enhancer warm, or allow it to cool and enjoy it chilled for a refreshing mood boost.

Variations

- For an iced tea version, let the infusion cool completely, then refrigerate for 1-2 hours. Serve over ice with a slice of lemon or orange for an extra vitamin C boost.

- Blend the cooled infusion with a handful of fresh berries for a fruity, antioxidant-rich mood enhancer.

- Add a slice of fresh ginger during the simmering process for its warming effects and additional anti-anxiety benefits.

Storage tips

Store any leftover Holy Basil Mood Enhancer in a sealed glass container in the refrigerator for up to 48 hours. Gently shake or stir before serving, as natural separation may occur.

Tips for allergens

For those with honey allergies or following a vegan diet, substitute honey with maple syrup or agave nectar to maintain the natural sweetness without using animal products. Ensure that the Holy Basil used is organic and free from pesticides to avoid potential allergens.

Skullcap Calming Tincture

Beneficial effects

Skullcap Calming Tincture is designed to naturally reduce anxiety and improve mood. Skullcap, a herb known for its sedative properties, can help calm the nervous system, making it an excellent remedy for stress and anxiety relief. Its active compounds, such as baicalin, have been shown to promote relaxation and support emotional well-being. Incorporating this tincture into your daily routine can aid in managing stress levels, enhancing overall mental clarity, and fostering a sense of calm.

Portions

Makes about 1 pint

Preparation time

10 minutes (plus 4-6 weeks for infusing)

Ingredients

- 4 ounces dried skullcap herb

- 1 pint (16 ounces) 100-proof vodka

Instructions

1. Begin by sourcing high-quality, organic dried skullcap herb to ensure the potency and purity of your tincture.
2. Place the dried skullcap in a clean, dry jar, such as a pint-sized mason jar.
3. Pour 1 pint of 100-proof vodka over the skullcap, making sure the herb is completely submerged in the alcohol. This ratio ensures optimal extraction of the skullcap's beneficial compounds.
4. Seal the jar tightly with a lid. Label the jar with the date and contents to keep track of the infusion time.
5. Store the jar in a cool, dark place, such as a cupboard or a pantry, away from direct sunlight. This environment is ideal for the infusion process.

6. Shake the jar gently once a day to mix the contents and facilitate the extraction of the skullcap's active ingredients into the vodka.
7. Allow the mixture to infuse for 4-6 weeks. The longer it infuses, the stronger and more potent the tincture will become.
8. After the infusion period, strain the tincture through a fine mesh strainer or cheesecloth into another clean, dry jar or bottle. Press or squeeze the skullcap to extract as much liquid as possible.
9. Transfer the strained tincture into dark glass dropper bottles for easy dosage and storage.

Variations

- To enhance the calming effects, consider adding other herbs known for their stress-relieving properties, such as chamomile or lavender, to the infusion.

- For a non-alcoholic version, glycerin can be used as a substitute for vodka, though the extraction process and shelf life may vary.

Storage tips

Store the Skullcap Calming Tincture in a cool, dark place, ideally in dark glass bottles to protect it from light degradation. Properly stored, the tincture can last for several years, maintaining its potency and effectiveness.

Tips for allergens

For individuals with allergies to alcohol, the glycerin-based tincture provides a viable alternative. Ensure the skullcap and any additional herbs used are sourced from reputable suppliers to avoid cross-contamination with allergens.

18.3: Natural Recipes for Infections and Inflammation

Turmeric and Honey Paste

Beneficial effects

Turmeric and Honey Paste combines the potent anti-inflammatory and antimicrobial properties of turmeric with the soothing and antibacterial effects of honey. This natural remedy is effective in treating infections, reducing inflammation, and accelerating the healing process of wounds. Curcumin, the active compound in turmeric, has been widely studied for its health benefits, including its ability to fight inflammation and support immune function. Honey, known for its wound-healing properties, acts as a natural preservative and sweetener, making the paste both beneficial and palatable.

Portions

Makes about 1/2 cup

Preparation time

5 minutes

Cooking time

No cooking required

Ingredients

- 1/4 cup turmeric powder

- 1/4 cup raw, organic honey

- 1 teaspoon black pepper (to enhance curcumin absorption)

- 2 tablespoons coconut oil (for its antimicrobial properties and to aid in absorption)

1. **Instructions**
2. In a clean, dry bowl, combine 1/4 cup of turmeric powder with 1/4 cup of raw, organic honey. Mix these ingredients until they form a consistent paste.
3. Add 1 teaspoon of freshly ground black pepper to the mixture. Black pepper contains piperine, which significantly enhances the absorption of curcumin by the body.
4. Incorporate 2 tablespoons of coconut oil into the paste. The coconut oil not only improves the texture and taste but also contributes additional antimicrobial benefits to the mixture.
5. Stir all the ingredients thoroughly until the mixture is smooth and evenly combined. Ensure there are no lumps in the paste.
6. Transfer the turmeric and honey paste into a clean, small glass jar with a tight-fitting lid. Press down on the paste with the back of a spoon to remove any air bubbles.

Variations

- For added health benefits, include a teaspoon of ground cinnamon to the mixture. Cinnamon can further enhance the anti-inflammatory and antimicrobial properties of the paste.

- If the taste of raw turmeric is too strong, add an extra tablespoon of honey to sweeten the paste further without compromising its health benefits.

Storage tips

Store the Turmeric and Honey Paste in a cool, dark place if using within a week. For longer storage, keep it refrigerated where it can last for up to 2-3 weeks. Ensure the jar is sealed tightly after each use to maintain freshness and prevent contamination.

Tips for allergens

Individuals with allergies to bee products can substitute honey with maple syrup, although this may alter the texture and antimicrobial properties of the paste. For those with coconut allergies, olive oil can be used as an alternative, providing a different but still healthful fat source.

Garlic and Olive Oil Infusion

Beneficial effects

Garlic and Olive Oil Infusion is a potent natural remedy known for its antibacterial, antiviral, and anti-inflammatory properties, making it an excellent choice for treating infections and reducing inflammation. Garlic contains allicin, a compound with significant therapeutic effects, including the ability to fight off pathogens and support immune function. Olive oil, rich in antioxidants and healthy fats, serves as an effective carrier oil, facilitating the absorption of garlic's beneficial compounds and providing additional anti-inflammatory benefits. This infusion can be used topically to address skin infections, ear infections, and as a gentle remedy for respiratory conditions when used as a chest rub.

Portions

Makes about 1 cup

Preparation time

10 minutes

Cooking time

2 hours (low heat infusion)

Ingredients

- 1 cup extra virgin olive oil

- 8 cloves of garlic, peeled and gently crushed

Instructions

1. Begin by sterilizing a glass jar and its lid by boiling them in water for 10 minutes. Carefully remove them using tongs and allow them to air dry on a clean towel.
2. Peel 8 cloves of garlic and gently crush them with the flat side of a knife to expose more surface area without completely mincing them. This process helps to release the allicin.
3. Place the crushed garlic cloves into the sterilized glass jar.
4. Pour 1 cup of extra virgin olive oil over the garlic cloves, ensuring they are completely submerged. Extra virgin olive oil is chosen for its high quality, antioxidant content, and mild flavor.
5. Seal the jar tightly with its lid.
6. To infuse the oil with garlic, place the sealed jar in a warm, sunny spot for 2 hours. Alternatively, for a gentler infusion, you can place the jar in a pot of warm water (not boiling), simulating a double boiler, and let it sit on the lowest heat setting for 2 hours. This method gently heats the oil, allowing the garlic's beneficial properties to infuse without degrading the oil or the garlic's active compounds.
7. After 2 hours, remove the jar from the heat source or sunny spot and let it cool to room temperature.
8. Strain the garlic oil infusion through a fine mesh strainer or cheesecloth into another sterilized jar to remove the garlic pieces. Press or squeeze the garlic in the strainer to extract as much oil as possible.
9. Discard the garlic solids and transfer the infused oil to a clean, sterilized bottle for storage.

Variations

- For added antimicrobial properties, you can include a few sprigs of fresh rosemary or thyme in the infusion.

- To enhance the infusion's anti-inflammatory effects, add a teaspoon of turmeric powder to the oil along with the garlic.

- For a warming effect, especially beneficial for chest rubs, include a small piece of ginger in the infusion process.

Storage tips

Store the Garlic and Olive Oil Infusion in a cool, dark place. If refrigerated, the olive oil may solidify but will return to liquid at room temperature. Use within one month for maximum potency.

Tips for allergens

For individuals with allergies to garlic, conducting a patch test on a small area of skin before widespread use is advisable. If any irritation occurs, discontinue use immediately.

Ginger and Turmeric Tea

Beneficial effects

Ginger and Turmeric Tea is a powerful anti-inflammatory and antioxidant-rich beverage, ideal for reducing inflammation and fighting infections. Turmeric contains curcumin, a compound with strong anti-inflammatory properties that can rival some anti-inflammatory drugs, without the side effects. Ginger, on the other hand, has been shown to significantly reduce body inflammation, help with pain relief, and support the immune system. Together, they create a potent natural remedy for soothing inflammation and bolstering the body's defenses against infections.

Portions

2 servings

Preparation time

5 minutes

Cooking time

10 minutes

Ingredients

- 1 inch fresh turmeric root, grated (or 1 teaspoon turmeric powder)

- 1 inch fresh ginger root, grated

- 4 cups water

- Honey to taste (optional)

- Juice of ½ lemon (optional)

Instructions

1. Bring 4 cups of water to a boil in a medium saucepan.
2. Add the grated turmeric and ginger to the boiling water. If using turmeric powder, ensure it's thoroughly dissolved.
3. Reduce the heat and simmer for 10 minutes to allow the turmeric and ginger to infuse their properties into the water.
4. After simmering, remove the saucepan from the heat.
5. Strain the tea through a fine mesh sieve into a large pitcher or directly into serving cups, discarding the solid pieces.
6. If desired, add honey to taste for sweetness and stir until dissolved.

7. Squeeze in the juice of ½ lemon to each serving for an added vitamin C boost and to enhance the tea's flavor.
8. Serve the tea warm to enjoy its full therapeutic benefits.

Variations

- For an added immune boost, include a pinch of black pepper with the turmeric and ginger. Black pepper increases the absorption of curcumin in the body.

- Add a cinnamon stick during the simmering process for additional anti-inflammatory benefits and a warming flavor.

- Mix in a tablespoon of apple cider vinegar to each serving for digestive support and an extra antimicrobial kick.

Storage tips

This tea is best enjoyed fresh, but you can store any leftovers in a sealed glass container in the refrigerator for up to 2 days. Reheat gently on the stove or enjoy cold, as preferred.

Tips for allergens

For those with allergies to honey, substitute it with maple syrup or simply omit it to enjoy the natural flavors of the tea. Ensure that the turmeric and ginger are sourced from reputable suppliers to avoid cross-contamination with allergens.

Chapter 19: Herbal Recipes by Type

19.1: Herbal Teas for Relaxation and Digestion

Lemon Verbena Relaxation Tea

Beneficial effects

Lemon Verbena Relaxation Tea is crafted to naturally alleviate stress and promote a sense of calm. Lemon Verbena, with its soothing aroma and flavor, has been traditionally used to reduce anxiety, improve sleep, and support digestive health. This herbal tea serves as a gentle remedy for unwinding after a busy day, aiding relaxation and enhancing overall well-being.

Portions

2 servings

Preparation time

5 minutes

Cooking time

10 minutes

Ingredients

- 2 tablespoons dried Lemon Verbena leaves

- 2 cups water

- Honey or lemon to taste (optional)

Instructions

1. Bring 2 cups of water to a boil in a medium saucepan.
2. Once boiling, remove the saucepan from the heat and add 2 tablespoons of dried Lemon Verbena leaves.
3. Cover the saucepan with a lid to prevent the escape of essential oils and allow the leaves to steep for 10 minutes.
4. After steeping, strain the tea through a fine mesh sieve into teacups, discarding the leaves.
5. If desired, enhance the flavor of the tea by adding honey or a squeeze of lemon to each cup according to taste. Stir well to ensure the added ingredients are fully dissolved.
6. Serve the Lemon Verbena Relaxation Tea warm to enjoy its maximum calming effects.

Variations

- For a refreshing twist, chill the tea in the refrigerator for an hour and serve over ice, garnishing with a slice of lemon or a sprig of fresh mint.

- Blend the tea with a handful of fresh berries for a fruity, antioxidant-rich version.

- Add a cinnamon stick during the steeping process for a warm, comforting flavor profile.

Storage tips

Store any leftover Lemon Verbena Relaxation Tea in a sealed glass container in the refrigerator for up to 2 days. Reheat gently on the stove or enjoy chilled, as preferred.

Tips for allergens

For those with honey allergies or following a vegan lifestyle, substitute honey with maple syrup or agave nectar to maintain the natural sweetness without using animal products. Ensure that the Lemon Verbena used is organic and free from pesticides to avoid potential allergens.

Ginger Chamomile Digestive Tea

Beneficial effects

Ginger Chamomile Digestive Tea is a soothing blend that combines the digestive benefits of ginger with the calming properties of chamomile. Ginger, known for its ability to alleviate gastrointestinal distress, can help reduce nausea, bloating, and gas. Chamomile, on the other hand, is celebrated for its gentle sedative effects, which can ease anxiety and promote relaxation, further aiding digestion. Together, they create a comforting tea that supports digestive health and encourages a sense of calm.

Portions

2 servings

Preparation time

5 minutes

Cooking time

10 minutes

Ingredients

- 1 tablespoon fresh ginger root, peeled and thinly sliced

- 2 tablespoons dried chamomile flowers

- 4 cups of water

- Honey or lemon to taste (optional)

Instructions

1. Begin by bringing 4 cups of water to a boil in a medium-sized saucepan.
2. While the water is heating, peel and thinly slice 1 tablespoon of fresh ginger root. The thin slices will ensure a stronger infusion of ginger's active compounds.
3. Once the water reaches a rolling boil, add the sliced ginger and 2 tablespoons of dried chamomile flowers to the saucepan.
4. Reduce the heat to low, allowing the tea to simmer gently for 10 minutes. This simmering process allows the ginger and chamomile to release their beneficial properties into the water.
5. After simmering, remove the saucepan from the heat. Strain the tea through a fine mesh sieve into a teapot or directly into serving cups, discarding the ginger slices and chamomile flowers.
6. If desired, enhance the flavor of the tea by adding honey or a squeeze of lemon according to taste. The honey can offer additional soothing properties for the throat, while lemon adds a refreshing tang and vitamin C.
7. Stir any added sweeteners or lemon juice until fully dissolved, then serve the tea warm to enjoy its digestive and calming benefits.

Variations

- For an extra digestive boost, add a pinch of peppermint leaves to the tea while it simmers. Peppermint can further aid in relieving digestive discomfort and adding a refreshing flavor.

- Incorporate a cinnamon stick during the simmering process for a subtly sweet and warming flavor, which can also support blood sugar regulation.

- To make a cold soothing beverage, allow the tea to cool completely, then refrigerate. Serve over ice for a refreshing digestive aid during warmer months.

Storage tips

This Ginger Chamomile Digestive Tea is best enjoyed fresh, but it can be stored in a sealed glass container in the refrigerator for up to 24 hours. Reheat gently on the stove or enjoy cold, as preferred.

Tips for allergens

For those with honey allergies or following a vegan diet, substitute honey with maple syrup or agave nectar to maintain the natural sweetness without using animal products. Ensure that the chamomile and ginger used are organic and free from pesticides to avoid potential allergens.

19.2: Tinctures and Tonics

Ginseng Detox Tonic

Beneficial effects

Ginseng Detox Tonic is designed to enhance the body's natural detoxification processes, boost energy levels, and support immune function. Ginseng, renowned for its adaptogenic properties, helps the body combat stress, fatigue, and enhances overall vitality. This tonic aids in flushing toxins from the body, promoting liver health, and improving circulation, making it an ideal beverage for those looking to cleanse their system and invigorate their health.

Portions

Makes about 4 cups

Preparation time

15 minutes

Ingredients

- 4 cups of filtered water

- 2 tablespoons of dried ginseng root

- 1 tablespoon of raw honey (optional, for sweetness)

- Juice of 1 lemon (for detoxification and to add a refreshing flavor)

- A pinch of cayenne pepper (to boost metabolism and circulation)

Instructions

1. Pour 4 cups of filtered water into a medium saucepan and bring to a gentle boil over medium heat.
2. Reduce the heat to low and add 2 tablespoons of dried ginseng root to the simmering water. Cover the saucepan with a lid and let simmer for 10 minutes, allowing the ginseng to steep and its properties to infuse into the water.
3. After 10 minutes, remove the saucepan from the heat and let it cool slightly for about 5 minutes.
4. Strain the tonic through a fine mesh sieve into a large pitcher or jar, discarding the ginseng roots.
5. Stir in 1 tablespoon of raw honey (if using) until it dissolves completely for a touch of natural sweetness.
6. Squeeze the juice of 1 lemon into the ginseng tonic, adding a refreshing flavor and enhancing its detoxifying benefits.
7. Add a pinch of cayenne pepper to the tonic and stir well. The cayenne pepper is optional but recommended for its metabolism-boosting and circulatory benefits.
8. Serve the tonic warm, or allow it to cool completely and enjoy it chilled for a refreshing detox beverage.

Variations

- For an added antioxidant boost, include a few slices of fresh ginger or turmeric root during the simmering process. Both ginger and turmeric are known for their anti-inflammatory and detoxifying properties.

- Replace honey with maple syrup for a vegan-friendly sweetener option.

- Add a sprig of fresh mint or a few slices of cucumber to the pitcher before chilling for a spa-like detox experience.

Storage tips

Store any leftover Ginseng Detox Tonic in a sealed glass container in the refrigerator for up to 3 days. Enjoy it cold or gently reheat on the stove for a warm tonic.

Tips for allergens

For those with allergies to honey, maple syrup or agave nectar are suitable alternatives that do not compromise the tonic's health benefits. Ensure that the ginseng root is sourced from a reputable supplier to avoid cross-contamination with allergens.

Dandelion Root Strengthening Tincture

Beneficial effects

Dandelion Root Strengthening Tincture harnesses the detoxifying and liver-supportive properties of dandelion root, making it an excellent tonic for enhancing the body's natural detoxification processes and strengthening overall vitality. Dandelion root is rich in antioxidants and compounds that promote liver health, aid in digestion, and support the elimination of toxins from the body. Regular use of this tincture can contribute to improved liver function, better digestion, and increased energy levels.

Portions

Makes about 1 pint

Preparation time

15 minutes (plus 4-6 weeks for infusing)

Ingredients

- 4 ounces dried dandelion root

- 1 pint (16 ounces) 100-proof vodka

Instructions

1. Begin by thoroughly cleaning and drying a pint-sized glass jar with a tight-fitting lid.
2. Measure 4 ounces of dried dandelion root and place it into the jar.
3. Pour 1 pint of 100-proof vodka over the dandelion root, ensuring the roots are completely submerged in the alcohol. The vodka acts as a solvent, extracting the beneficial compounds from the dandelion root.
4. Seal the jar tightly and shake it gently to mix the dandelion root with the vodka.
5. Label the jar with the current date and contents, noting the "Dandelion Root Strengthening Tincture" for easy identification.
6. Store the jar in a cool, dark place, such as a cupboard or a pantry, away from direct sunlight and temperature fluctuations.
7. Shake the jar gently once a day to facilitate the extraction process.
8. After 4-6 weeks, strain the tincture through a fine mesh strainer or cheesecloth into a clean, dark glass bottle. Press or squeeze the dandelion root to extract as much liquid as possible.
9. Discard the used dandelion root.
10. Label the bottle with the name of the tincture and the date of straining. Store the tincture in a cool, dark place.

Variations

- To enhance the tonic's detoxifying effects, consider adding 1 tablespoon of milk thistle seeds to the jar along with the dandelion root before adding the vodka.

- For a slightly sweeter tincture that may be more palatable when taken directly, add a few slices of fresh organic lemon or a teaspoon of raw honey to the jar during the infusing process.

Storage tips

Store the finished tincture in a cool, dark place. The tincture will remain potent for up to 3 years if stored properly. Ensure the bottle is tightly sealed to prevent evaporation and degradation of the active compounds.

Tips for allergens

For individuals sensitive to alcohol, the tincture can be evaporated slightly before use by adding the desired amount to hot water, allowing the alcohol to evaporate and leaving the beneficial compounds of the dandelion root. Always consult with a healthcare provider before starting any new herbal supplement, especially if you have allergies, are pregnant, nursing, or taking medication.

19.3: Infused Oils and Salves

All-Purpose Herbal Salve

Beneficial effects

The All-Purpose Herbal Salve is a versatile, natural remedy designed to soothe, protect, and heal minor cuts, scrapes, burns, and dry skin. Its blend of healing herbs and oils offers anti-inflammatory, antibacterial, and antiseptic properties, making it an essential addition to any home apothecary. This salve can help accelerate the healing process, reduce the risk of infection, and provide a protective barrier to aid skin recovery.

Portions

Makes approximately 8 ounces

Preparation time

20 minutes

Cooking time

1 hour

Ingredients

- 1/2 cup coconut oil
- 1/2 cup olive oil
- 1/4 cup dried calendula petals
- 1/4 cup dried comfrey leaves
- 1/4 cup dried plantain leaves
- 2 tablespoons beeswax pellets
- 10 drops lavender essential oil
- 10 drops tea tree essential oil

Instructions

1. Combine coconut oil and olive oil in a double boiler over low heat.
2. Add dried calendula petals, comfrey leaves, and plantain leaves to the oils. Stir gently to ensure the herbs are fully submerged.
3. Simmer the herb and oil mixture on low heat for 1 hour, stirring occasionally. This slow infusion process extracts the healing properties of the herbs into the oils.
4. After 1 hour, carefully strain the oil through a cheesecloth or fine mesh strainer into a clean bowl, pressing the herbs to extract as much oil as possible. Discard the used herbs.
5. Return the strained oil to the double boiler and add beeswax pellets. Stir continuously over low heat until the beeswax is completely melted and combined with the herbal oil.
6. Remove from heat and let the mixture cool for a few minutes, but not solidify.
7. Stir in lavender and tea tree essential oils for their additional healing and aromatic properties.

8. Carefully pour the liquid salve into clean, dry tins or jars. Allow to cool and solidify completely at room temperature.

9. Once solidified, seal the containers with lids to preserve the salve.

Variations

- For extra moisturizing properties, add a tablespoon of shea butter to the oil mixture before adding beeswax.

- Substitute chamomile for calendula for a salve with calming skin properties, ideal for sensitive or irritated skin.

- For a vegan version, use candelilla wax instead of beeswax, adjusting the quantity as needed to achieve the desired consistency.

Storage tips

Store the All-Purpose Herbal Salve in a cool, dry place away from direct sunlight. If stored properly, the salve can last for up to 1 year. Keep the salve in airtight containers to maintain its potency and prevent contamination.

Tips for allergens

For individuals with sensitivities to lavender or tea tree oil, omit these essential oils or substitute with another skin-friendly essential oil like chamomile or rosehip. Always conduct a patch test on a small area of skin before applying broadly, especially if you have sensitive skin or known allergies.

Arnica Salve

Beneficial effects

Arnica Salve is renowned for its ability to reduce inflammation and alleviate pain, making it an essential remedy for bruises, sprains, and muscle soreness. The active compounds in arnica, such as helenalin and flavonoids, contribute to its anti-inflammatory and analgesic properties. This salve can promote healing by improving blood circulation to the affected area, reducing swelling, and speeding up the recovery process. It's particularly beneficial for athletes, individuals with arthritis, and those recovering from minor injuries.

Portions

Makes about 8 ounces

Preparation time

15 minutes

Cooking time

30 minutes

Ingredients

- 1/2 cup arnica montana flowers (dried)

- 1 cup olive oil or coconut oil (as a base)

- 1/4 cup beeswax pellets (to thicken the salve)

- 10 drops lavender essential oil (for additional anti-inflammatory and soothing effects)

- 5 drops peppermint essential oil (for a cooling sensation and to enhance pain relief)

Instructions

1. Begin by placing the dried arnica montana flowers in a clean, dry jar.
2. Pour 1 cup of olive oil or coconut oil over the flowers, ensuring they are completely submerged. Seal the jar tightly.
3. Create a double boiler by filling a pot with water, about a quarter full, and placing it on the stove over medium heat. Place the jar in the pot, making sure water does not enter the jar.
4. Allow the oil and arnica mixture to infuse over low heat for 3 hours, ensuring the water does not boil. Stir occasionally and check to ensure the oil does not overheat.
5. After 3 hours, carefully remove the jar from the heat and let it cool slightly. Strain the oil through a cheesecloth or fine mesh strainer into a clean bowl, discarding the arnica flowers.
6. Add the beeswax pellets to the infused oil. If necessary, return the mixture to the double boiler, stirring until the beeswax is completely melted and combined with the oil.
7. Remove from heat and stir in the lavender and peppermint essential oils.
8. Quickly pour the mixture into small tins or glass jars before it begins to solidify. Let them cool at room temperature.
9. Once solidified, seal the containers with lids to preserve the salve.

Variations

- For extra skin nourishment, add a tablespoon of vitamin E oil to the mixture after removing it from heat. Vitamin E can help moisturize the skin and improve the salve's shelf life.

- Substitute olive or coconut oil with almond oil for a lighter texture that's easily absorbed by the skin.

- For a vegan version, use candelilla wax instead of beeswax, using about half the amount recommended for beeswax.

Storage tips

Store the Arnica Salve in a cool, dark place. If stored properly, the salve can last for up to a year. Avoid exposing it to direct sunlight or heat as it can cause the salve to melt.

Tips for allergens

For those allergic to beeswax, candelilla wax is a suitable plant-based alternative. Always perform a patch test before applying the salve extensively, especially if you have sensitive skin or are prone to allergies. If using a new batch of essential oils, test them separately as they can be potent allergens for some individuals.

19.4: Immune-Boosting Syrups and Honeys

Elderberry Immune Boosting Syrup

Beneficial effects

Elderberry Immune Boosting Syrup is a potent remedy known for its antiviral and immune-enhancing properties. Rich in antioxidants and vitamins that can help fight off colds and flu, elderberry syrup provides a natural method for boosting the immune system. Studies have shown that elderberry can reduce the duration and severity of symptoms when taken at the onset of cold or flu.

Portions

Makes approximately 16 ounces

Preparation time

15 minutes

Cooking time

45 minutes

Ingredients

- 3/4 cup dried elderberries
- 3 cups water
- 1 teaspoon dried ginger
- 1 teaspoon cinnamon
- 1/2 teaspoon cloves
- 1 cup raw honey

Instructions

1. Combine 3/4 cup of dried elderberries with 3 cups of water in a medium saucepan. Add 1 teaspoon of dried ginger, 1 teaspoon of cinnamon, and 1/2 teaspoon of cloves to the saucepan.
2. Bring the mixture to a boil, then reduce the heat and allow it to simmer for about 45 minutes, or until the liquid has reduced by half.
3. Remove the saucepan from the heat and let the mixture cool until it is warm to the touch.
4. Mash the elderberries gently using a spoon or a potato masher to release any remaining juice.
5. Strain the mixture through a fine mesh strainer or cheesecloth into a large bowl, pressing on the elderberry solids to extract as much liquid as possible. Discard the solids.
6. Once the liquid has cooled to lukewarm, stir in 1 cup of raw honey until it is fully dissolved. It's important to add the honey after the liquid has cooled to preserve its natural enzymes and benefits.
7. Pour the finished syrup into sterilized glass bottles or jars. Seal the containers with lids.

Variations

- For an extra immune boost, add a tablespoon of fresh grated ginger or turmeric to the mixture while simmering.

- Substitute raw honey with maple syrup for a vegan-friendly version.

- Add a squeeze of fresh lemon juice after the syrup has cooled for added vitamin C and a tangy flavor.

Storage tips

Store the Elderberry Immune Boosting Syrup in the refrigerator for up to two months. For longer storage, the syrup can be frozen in ice cube trays and then transferred to a freezer-safe container for easy dosing.

Tips for allergens

For those with allergies to honey, maple syrup is a suitable alternative that still provides natural sweetness and additional health benefits. Ensure that all spices used are organic to avoid potential contaminants.

Ginger-Honey Cough Relief Syrup

Beneficial effects

Ginger-Honey Cough Relief Syrup is a natural remedy designed to soothe sore throats, reduce coughing, and boost the immune system. Ginger, with its anti-inflammatory properties, helps to relieve irritation in the throat, while honey acts as a natural cough suppressant and antibacterial agent, coating the throat to ease discomfort. This syrup is an effective, gentle option for those seeking relief from cough and cold symptoms using ingredients from their kitchen.

Portions

Makes about 1 cup

Preparation time

5 minutes

Cooking time

20 minutes

Ingredients

- 1 cup raw, organic honey

- 1/4 cup fresh ginger root, finely grated

- 2 tablespoons lemon juice

- 1/4 cup filtered water

- 1/2 teaspoon ground cinnamon (optional for additional flavor and benefits)

Instructions

1. Combine 1/4 cup of finely grated fresh ginger root with 1/4 cup of filtered water in a small saucepan. Bring the mixture to a simmer over medium heat, then reduce the heat to low and continue to simmer for 10 minutes. This process extracts the beneficial compounds from the ginger.
2. Strain the ginger water through a fine mesh sieve into a bowl, pressing on the ginger to extract as much liquid as possible. Discard the ginger solids.

3. Return the ginger-infused water to the saucepan and add 1 cup of raw, organic honey. Warm the mixture over low heat, stirring constantly, until the honey is fully dissolved into the ginger water. Do not allow the mixture to boil to preserve the beneficial enzymes in the honey.
4. Remove the saucepan from the heat and stir in 2 tablespoons of lemon juice. The lemon juice adds vitamin C and enhances the syrup's flavor.
5. If using, sprinkle in 1/2 teaspoon of ground cinnamon and stir well. Cinnamon adds a warming effect and additional anti-inflammatory benefits.
6. Allow the syrup to cool to room temperature. Once cooled, pour the syrup into a clean, dry glass jar with a tight-fitting lid.

Variations

- For an extra immune boost, add a teaspoon of ground turmeric to the ginger water while simmering. Turmeric's curcumin content offers potent anti-inflammatory and antioxidant benefits.

- Incorporate a few cloves or a star anise into the simmering ginger water for added depth of flavor and additional antimicrobial properties.

- Substitute lemon juice with orange juice for a different citrus twist that still provides vitamin C and a sweet flavor.

Storage tips

Store the Ginger-Honey Cough Relief Syrup in the refrigerator in an airtight glass jar. The syrup can be kept for up to 2 months. Always use a clean spoon when serving to maintain its purity and extend its shelf life.

Tips for allergens

For those with allergies to honey, a high-quality agave syrup can be used as an alternative, though the antimicrobial properties may vary. If you're sensitive to ginger, start with a smaller amount and adjust according to your tolerance.

19.5: DIY Beauty and Self-Care

Aloe Vera and Coconut Oil Moisturizer

Beneficial effects

Aloe Vera and Coconut Oil Moisturizer harnesses the hydrating power of aloe vera, combined with the nourishing benefits of coconut oil, to create a natural, soothing moisturizer. Aloe vera is renowned for its ability to soothe burns, hydrate the skin, and reduce inflammation, making it an ideal ingredient for skin care. Coconut oil, rich in fatty acids, antioxidants, and antimicrobial properties, deeply nourishes the skin, locks in moisture, and protects against harmful bacteria. Together, these ingredients create a powerful moisturizer that promotes healthy, radiant skin.

Portions

Makes about 8 ounces

Preparation time

10 minutes

Cooking time

No cooking required

Ingredients

- 1/2 cup pure aloe vera gel

- 1/4 cup coconut oil, solid at room temperature

- 10 drops lavender essential oil (for its calming and anti-inflammatory properties)

- 5 drops vitamin E oil (as a natural preservative and skin conditioner)

Instructions

1. In a mixing bowl, combine 1/2 cup of pure aloe vera gel with 1/4 cup of solid coconut oil. Use a hand mixer or whisk to blend the ingredients together until a smooth, creamy consistency is achieved.
2. Once the aloe vera and coconut oil are thoroughly mixed, add 10 drops of lavender essential oil to the mixture. Lavender oil not only adds a soothing fragrance but also enhances the moisturizer's skin-calming benefits.
3. Incorporate 5 drops of vitamin E oil into the blend. Vitamin E acts as a natural antioxidant, helping to prolong the shelf life of the moisturizer while nourishing the skin.
4. Continue to mix for an additional minute to ensure all the oils are evenly distributed throughout the moisturizer.
5. Transfer the finished moisturizer into a clean, dry glass jar or an airtight container. Seal the container to prevent contamination and preserve the moisturizer's freshness.

Variations

- For a rejuvenating boost, add a few drops of rosehip oil to the mixture. Rosehip oil is rich in vitamins and antioxidants, promoting skin regeneration and improving skin texture.

- If you prefer a thicker consistency, increase the amount of coconut oil to 1/3 cup. For a lighter moisturizer, especially suitable for oily skin types, reduce the coconut oil to 2 tablespoons.

- Customize the scent by substituting lavender essential oil with another skin-friendly essential oil such as chamomile or tea tree oil, depending on your skin's needs and your scent preference.

Storage tips

Store the Aloe Vera and Coconut Oil Moisturizer in a cool, dry place, away from direct sunlight. If stored properly in an airtight container, the moisturizer can last for up to 3 months. For extended freshness, consider refrigerating the moisturizer, especially in warmer climates.

Tips for allergens

For individuals with sensitivities to coconut oil, jojoba oil or almond oil can be used as effective alternatives. If allergic to lavender essential oil, omit it or choose a hypoallergenic essential oil that suits your skin type and preferences. Always conduct a patch test on a small area of skin before applying the moisturizer extensively.

Honey and Avocado Hair Mask

Beneficial effects

The Honey and Avocado Hair Mask is a deeply nourishing treatment that leverages the natural moisturizing properties of honey and the rich vitamins and healthy fats found in avocado. This combination is excellent for restoring hydration to dry, damaged hair, promoting scalp health, and adding a natural shine to your locks. Honey acts as a humectant, drawing moisture into the hair, while avocado provides essential nutrients like vitamins A, E, and D, and omega-3 fatty acids, which help to repair hair damage and prevent future breakage.

Portions

Enough for 2-3 applications, depending on hair length and thickness

Preparation time

10 minutes

Ingredients

- 1 ripe avocado

- 2 tablespoons of raw, organic honey

- 1 tablespoon of coconut oil (optional, for extra moisture)

- 1 teaspoon of lemon juice (optional, to help balance scalp pH)

Instructions

1. Start by cutting the avocado in half, removing the pit, and scooping the flesh into a mixing bowl.
2. Mash the avocado with a fork or potato masher until it reaches a smooth consistency with minimal lumps.
3. Add 2 tablespoons of raw, organic honey to the mashed avocado. If your honey is solidified, gently warm it in a water bath or microwave for a few seconds until it becomes runny, but not hot.
4. (Optional) For additional moisture, especially beneficial for very dry or curly hair types, mix in 1 tablespoon of coconut oil. If the coconut oil is solid, warm it slightly until it liquefies before adding.
5. (Optional) To help balance the scalp's pH and add a fresh scent to the mask, stir in 1 teaspoon of lemon juice.
6. Once all the ingredients are combined, apply the mask to damp hair, starting from the roots and working down to the tips. Ensure that every strand is coated.
7. Cover your hair with a shower cap or wrap it in a warm towel to help the nutrients penetrate more deeply.
8. Leave the mask on for at least 20 minutes. For deeper conditioning, you can leave it on for up to an hour.
9. Rinse the mask out with lukewarm water, then shampoo and condition as usual.

Variations

- For an extra protein boost, add an egg yolk to the mixture before applying. This can help strengthen hair prone to breakage.

- Incorporate a few drops of essential oils like lavender or rosemary for their additional scalp benefits and soothing fragrance.

- Replace coconut oil with olive oil for a lighter alternative that still offers excellent moisturizing properties.

Storage tips

It's best to prepare the Honey and Avocado Hair Mask fresh for each use, as the avocado may brown and lose its potency when stored. However, any leftover mask can be stored in the refrigerator for up to 24 hours. Be sure to cover it tightly to prevent oxidation.

Tips for allergens

For those allergic to citrus, omit the lemon juice to avoid any scalp irritation. If you're sensitive to coconut oil, olive oil is a great alternative that's less likely to cause any adverse reactions. Always patch test the mask on a small section of your scalp before full application, especially if you decide to add essential oils.

Green Tea and Chamomile Face Toner

Beneficial effects

Green Tea and Chamomile Face Toner combines the antioxidant-rich properties of green tea with the soothing effects of chamomile to create a gentle yet effective toner for all skin types. Green tea is known for its ability to reduce inflammation, combat acne, and provide anti-aging benefits by protecting the skin from free radical damage. Chamomile, renowned for its calming properties, helps to soothe irritated skin, reduce redness, and promote a healthy, radiant complexion. Together, they create a toner that balances the skin's natural oils, tightens pores, and leaves the skin feeling refreshed and revitalized.

Portions

Makes about 8 ounces

Preparation time

10 minutes

Cooking time

5 minutes

Ingredients

- 1/2 cup distilled water

- 1/2 cup brewed green tea (cooled)

- 2 tablespoons dried chamomile flowers or 1 chamomile tea bag

- 1 tablespoon witch hazel

- 1 teaspoon aloe vera gel

- 5 drops lavender essential oil (optional for additional soothing properties)

Instructions

1. Begin by brewing 1/2 cup of green tea. Allow it to cool to room temperature.
2. In a small saucepan, bring 1/2 cup of distilled water to a simmer. Add 2 tablespoons of dried chamomile flowers or 1 chamomile tea bag to the simmering water. Remove from heat and let steep for 5 minutes.
3. Strain the chamomile infusion into a bowl, removing all solid particles.
4. Combine the cooled green tea and chamomile infusion in a glass measuring cup or bowl.
5. Add 1 tablespoon of witch hazel to the tea mixture. Witch hazel acts as a natural astringent, helping to tighten pores and smooth the skin's appearance.
6. Stir in 1 teaspoon of aloe vera gel for its hydrating and healing properties.
7. If using, add 5 drops of lavender essential oil to the mixture for its calming and anti-inflammatory benefits.
8. Pour the toner into a clean, sterilized glass bottle with a tight-fitting lid or spray top.
9. To use, apply the toner to a cotton pad and gently swipe across clean, dry skin. Alternatively, spray directly onto the face with eyes closed. Use morning and night for best results.

Variations

- For oily skin, add a teaspoon of apple cider vinegar to the mixture to help balance the skin's pH and control excess oil production.

- For extra hydration, dissolve a teaspoon of honey in the warm chamomile infusion before combining it with the green tea. Honey is a natural humectant that helps the skin retain moisture.

- Replace lavender essential oil with tea tree essential oil for added antibacterial properties, beneficial for acne-prone skin.

Storage tips

Store the Green Tea and Chamomile Face Toner in the refrigerator to preserve its freshness and extend its shelf life. Use within 2 weeks for optimal benefits.

Tips for allergens

For those with sensitivities to essential oils, omit the lavender essential oil or substitute it with a milder oil, such as rosehip, which is also beneficial for the skin but less likely to cause irritation. Always conduct a patch test on the inner arm before applying new products to the face, especially for those with sensitive skin.

Chapter 20: Seasonal Apothecary

20.1: Spring Detox Remedies

Dandelion-Nettle Infusion

Beneficial effects

Dandelion-Nettle Infusion is a powerful detoxifying beverage, ideal for springtime rejuvenation. Dandelion root is celebrated for its liver-supportive and diuretic properties, aiding in the elimination of toxins from the body. Nettle, rich in vitamins A, C, and iron, supports kidney function and provides a boost to the immune system. Together, these herbs create a potent drink that not only detoxifies but also replenishes essential nutrients, promoting overall health and vitality.

Portions

Makes about 4 cups

Preparation time

10 minutes

Cooking time

15 minutes

Ingredients

- 1/4 cup dried dandelion root

- 1/4 cup dried nettle leaves

- 4 cups water

- Honey or lemon to taste (optional)

Instructions

1. Bring 4 cups of water to a boil in a large saucepan.
2. Reduce the heat to low and add 1/4 cup of dried dandelion root and 1/4 cup of dried nettle leaves to the simmering water.
3. Cover the saucepan with a lid and let the mixture simmer for 15 minutes, allowing the herbs to steep and their beneficial compounds to infuse into the water.
4. After 15 minutes, remove the saucepan from the heat and let it cool slightly for about 5 minutes, making it safe to handle.
5. Strain the infusion through a fine mesh sieve into a large pitcher or jar, pressing on the herbs to extract as much liquid as possible. Discard the used herbs.
6. If desired, enhance the flavor of the infusion by adding honey or a squeeze of lemon according to taste. Stir well to ensure any added sweeteners are fully dissolved.
7. Serve the Dandelion-Nettle Infusion warm, or allow it to cool completely and enjoy it chilled for a refreshing detox beverage.

Variations

- For an added boost of flavor and antioxidants, include a few slices of fresh ginger or a cinnamon stick to the water while simmering the dandelion and nettle.

- Incorporate a tablespoon of fresh mint leaves to the infusion after removing it from heat for a refreshing, digestive aid.

- Replace honey with maple syrup for a vegan-friendly sweetener option that complements the earthy tones of the dandelion and nettle.

Storage tips

Store any leftover Dandelion-Nettle Infusion in a sealed glass container in the refrigerator for up to 48 hours. Enjoy it cold or gently reheat on the stove for a warm, detoxifying drink.

Tips for allergens

For those with allergies to honey, maple syrup or agave nectar are suitable alternatives that still provide natural sweetness without the allergens. Ensure that the dandelion and nettle are sourced from reputable suppliers to avoid cross-contamination with allergens.

Lemon-Ginger Detox Drink

Beneficial effects

Lemon-Ginger Detox Drink is designed to support the body's natural detoxification processes, stimulate digestion, and boost the immune system. The ginger in this drink offers powerful anti-inflammatory and antioxidant properties, aiding in the reduction of inflammation and the neutralization of harmful free radicals. Lemon, rich in vitamin C, not only enhances the immune system but also supports liver function, a key organ in the body's detoxification process. Together, these ingredients create a refreshing beverage that can help to cleanse the system, improve energy levels, and promote overall well-being.

Portions

2 servings

Preparation time

10 minutes

Cooking time

No cooking required

Ingredients

- 1 inch fresh ginger root, peeled and thinly sliced

- Juice of 1 large lemon

- 2 cups of filtered water

- 1 tablespoon raw honey (optional)

- A pinch of cayenne pepper (optional, for an extra detoxifying boost)

Instructions

1. Start by peeling and thinly slicing 1 inch of fresh ginger root. The thin slices will ensure maximum extraction of ginger's beneficial compounds.
2. In a large pitcher, combine the sliced ginger with the juice of 1 large lemon. Lemon juice not only adds a refreshing taste but also contributes to the detoxifying effects of the drink.
3. Add 2 cups of filtered water to the pitcher. Stir well to combine the ingredients.
4. If desired, add 1 tablespoon of raw honey to the mixture. Honey can sweeten the drink and add its own antioxidant properties, but it's optional based on personal preference for sweetness.
5. For those looking for an extra detoxifying boost, add a pinch of cayenne pepper to the mixture. Cayenne pepper is known for its ability to stimulate circulation and aid in the elimination of toxins.
6. Stir the mixture thoroughly until all the ingredients are well combined.
7. Refrigerate the drink for at least 30 minutes to allow the flavors to meld and the ginger to infuse into the water.
8. Serve the Lemon-Ginger Detox Drink chilled. Before serving, you can strain the drink to remove the ginger slices, or leave them in for added flavor and benefits.

Variations

- For an added health kick, include a few slices of cucumber or a handful of fresh mint leaves to the pitcher before refrigerating. Both add a refreshing twist and additional detoxifying properties.

- Replace filtered water with sparkling water for a fizzy variation that's both refreshing and beneficial.

- For those who prefer a warmer beverage, this drink can also be enjoyed heated. Simply warm the mixture gently on the stove without boiling, to preserve the nutrients in the honey and lemon.

Storage tips

The Lemon-Ginger Detox Drink is best enjoyed fresh but can be stored in the refrigerator for up to 2 days. Keep it in a sealed pitcher or bottle to maintain its freshness and prevent absorption of other flavors from the fridge.

Tips for allergens

For individuals with allergies to honey, the sweetener can be omitted or replaced with maple syrup for a similar sweetness without the allergenic concern. Always ensure fresh ingredients are used to avoid potential contaminants.

20.2: Summer Skin Protection Remedies

Aloe-Lavender Gel

Beneficial effects

Aloe-Lavender Gel combines the soothing, hydrating properties of aloe vera with the calming, anti-inflammatory benefits of lavender essential oil. Aloe vera, known for its ability to treat sunburns, moisturizes and heals the skin without leaving a greasy residue. Lavender essential oil provides a gentle soothing effect, reducing inflammation and redness, making this gel perfect for after-sun care or to calm irritated skin. Together, these ingredients create a cooling, therapeutic gel that promotes skin healing and relaxation.

Portions

Enough for approximately 10 applications

Preparation time

10 minutes

Ingredients

- 1 cup pure aloe vera gel

- 10 drops lavender essential oil

- 2 tablespoons vitamin E oil

- 1/4 cup distilled water (optional, for a thinner consistency)

Instructions

1. In a clean mixing bowl, add 1 cup of pure aloe vera gel. Ensure the aloe vera gel is cold-pressed and free from added colors or fragrances for maximum benefits.
2. To the aloe vera gel, carefully add 10 drops of lavender essential oil. Choose a therapeutic-grade essential oil to ensure purity and effectiveness.
3. Incorporate 2 tablespoons of vitamin E oil into the mixture. Vitamin E oil acts as a natural preservative and helps to nourish and protect the skin further.
4. (Optional) For those preferring a thinner consistency, gradually mix in 1/4 cup of distilled water to the aloe-lavender mixture. Stir continuously to achieve a uniform gel.
5. Using a whisk or an electric mixer, blend all ingredients on low speed until fully combined and the mixture achieves a smooth, gel-like consistency.
6. Transfer the aloe-lavender gel into a clean, sterilized glass jar or a squeeze bottle for easy application. Ensure the container has been sterilized to prevent contamination.
7. Label the container with the contents and date of creation.

Variations

- For additional cooling effects, add 5 drops of peppermint essential oil to the gel. Peppermint provides a refreshing sensation, ideal for hot summer days or after sun exposure.

- To enhance the gel's skin-soothing properties, mix in 1 tablespoon of chamomile tea (cooled) in place of distilled water. Chamomile has anti-inflammatory properties, making it excellent for sensitive or irritated skin.

- For a hydrating boost, incorporate 1 tablespoon of glycerin into the gel. Glycerin helps draw moisture into the skin, enhancing the hydrating effects of aloe vera.

Storage tips

Store the aloe-lavender gel in the refrigerator to maintain its freshness and enhance the cooling effect upon application. The gel can be kept for up to 1 month when stored properly in the fridge. Always use clean hands or a spatula to scoop out the gel to prevent bacterial contamination.

Tips for allergens

For those with sensitivities to lavender, the essential oil can be omitted or replaced with another skin-friendly essential oil like rose or chamomile essential oil. Always perform a patch test on a small area of skin before widespread use, especially if incorporating new or additional essential oils.

Calendula-Chamomile Lotion

Beneficial effects

Calendula-Chamomile Lotion is designed to soothe and protect the skin during the summer months, leveraging the anti-inflammatory and healing properties of calendula and the calming effects of chamomile. This natural lotion can help alleviate sunburn, reduce inflammation, and moisturize dry skin, making it an ideal choice for after-sun care. Calendula, known for its ability to heal wounds and hydrate the skin, works in synergy with chamomile, which soothes irritated skin and promotes relaxation with its gentle scent.

Portions

Makes approximately 8 ounces

Preparation time

15 minutes

Cooking time

10 minutes

Ingredients

- 1/4 cup dried calendula petals

- 1/4 cup dried chamomile flowers

- 1/2 cup coconut oil

- 1/4 cup shea butter

- 2 tablespoons beeswax pellets

- 1/2 cup aloe vera gel

- 10 drops lavender essential oil

Instructions

1. Begin by infusing the coconut oil with calendula and chamomile. Combine the dried calendula petals and chamomile flowers with the coconut oil in a double boiler. Heat gently over low heat for 30 minutes to allow the herbs to infuse their properties into the oil.
2. After 30 minutes, strain the oil through a cheesecloth or fine mesh strainer to remove the herb particles. Discard the herbs and return the infused oil to the double boiler.
3. Add shea butter and beeswax pellets to the infused oil in the double boiler. Stir continuously until the shea butter and beeswax have melted completely and are well combined with the oil.
4. Remove the mixture from heat and let it cool for a few minutes until it's warm but not set.
5. Slowly stir in the aloe vera gel and lavender essential oil into the warm oil mixture. Mix thoroughly to ensure a smooth, homogenous lotion.

6. Pour the lotion into a clean, dry container while it's still liquid. Allow it to cool and solidify at room temperature.

7. Once cooled and solidified, seal the container with a lid to preserve the lotion.

Variations

- For extra cooling effects, especially beneficial after sun exposure, add a few drops of peppermint essential oil to the lotion.

- If you prefer a vegan option, substitute beeswax pellets with candelilla wax, using half the amount recommended for beeswax.

- For an antioxidant boost, incorporate a teaspoon of vitamin E oil into the lotion as it cools, before it solidifies.

Storage tips

Store the Calendula-Chamomile Lotion in a cool, dry place away from direct sunlight. If stored properly in an airtight container, the lotion can last for up to 6 months. For best results, keep it in the refrigerator during the hot summer months to maintain its soothing, cool effect upon application.

Tips for allergens

For individuals sensitive to lavender, omit the essential oil or substitute with another skin-friendly essential oil like rosehip or chamomile. Always conduct a patch test on a small area of skin before applying the lotion extensively, especially if you have sensitive skin or known allergies.

20.3: Autumn Immunity Boosters

Rosehip Immune Elixir

Beneficial effects

Rosehip Immune Elixir is a potent concoction designed to bolster the immune system, particularly beneficial during the autumn months when the risk of colds and flu increases. Rosehips, the fruit of the rose plant, are a powerhouse of vitamin C, antioxidants, and polyphenols that help to strengthen the body's defenses against infections. Regular consumption of this elixir can aid in reducing inflammation, fighting off viruses, and improving overall health and vitality.

Portions

Makes about 2 cups

Preparation time

10 minutes

Cooking time

No cooking required

Ingredients

- 1 cup dried rosehips

- 2 cups boiling water

- 1 tablespoon raw honey (optional, for sweetness)

- Juice of 1 lemon (to enhance vitamin C content and add flavor)

- 1 inch piece of ginger, grated (for additional immune support and warmth)

Instructions

1. Place 1 cup of dried rosehips in a heat-resistant glass jar or pitcher.
2. Pour 2 cups of boiling water over the rosehips, ensuring they are completely submerged.
3. Cover the jar or pitcher and let the rosehips steep for at least 4 hours, or overnight for a stronger infusion. This long steeping time allows for the maximum extraction of the rosehips' beneficial properties.
4. After steeping, strain the liquid through a fine mesh sieve or cheesecloth into another jar, pressing on the rosehips to extract as much liquid as possible. Discard the rosehips.
5. Stir in 1 tablespoon of raw honey (if using) until fully dissolved. The honey adds a natural sweetness and additional antibacterial properties to the elixir.
6. Add the juice of 1 lemon to the rosehip infusion, providing a refreshing taste and boosting the vitamin C content.
7. Grate 1 inch piece of ginger and squeeze the juice into the elixir for an extra layer of immune support and a warming effect.
8. Mix all the ingredients thoroughly until well combined.
9. The Rosehip Immune Elixir is now ready to be consumed. Enjoy it chilled or at room temperature for best results.

Variations

- For an extra antioxidant boost, add a cinnamon stick to the jar while the rosehips are steeping.

- Incorporate a pinch of turmeric powder to the elixir for its anti-inflammatory benefits and to enhance the immune-boosting effects.

- Replace honey with maple syrup for a vegan-friendly sweetener that complements the tangy flavor of the rosehips.

Storage tips

Keep the Rosehip Immune Elixir refrigerated in a sealed glass container. Consume within 5 days for optimal freshness and potency. Shake well before each use as natural settling may occur.

Tips for allergens

Individuals with allergies to honey can substitute it with agave syrup or simply omit the sweetener. For those sensitive to citrus, the lemon juice can be reduced or replaced with a splash of apple cider vinegar for a similar acidic balance without the allergen concern.

Turmeric Immune Paste

Beneficial effects

Turmeric Immune Paste is a concentrated blend designed to enhance the body's immune response and provide anti-inflammatory benefits. Turmeric, the main ingredient, contains curcumin, a compound with potent antioxidant and anti-inflammatory properties that can help reduce inflammation and boost immunity. This paste also aids in improving digestion, which is crucial for maintaining a strong immune system, as a significant portion of the body's immune system is located in the gut.

Portions

Makes about 1 cup

Preparation time

10 minutes

Ingredients

- 1/2 cup turmeric powder

- 1 cup water

- 1/4 cup raw, organic honey

- 2 tablespoons coconut oil

- 1 1/2 teaspoons black pepper

Instructions

1. In a small pot, combine 1/2 cup of turmeric powder with 1 cup of water. Stir well to ensure the turmeric is fully dissolved in the water.
2. Place the pot over low heat and simmer the mixture, stirring constantly, for 7-10 minutes until it forms a thick paste. Adjust the heat as necessary to prevent the mixture from boiling.
3. Remove the pot from the heat. Let the turmeric paste cool down for a few minutes until it is warm to the touch but not hot.
4. Stir in 1/4 cup of raw, organic honey into the warm turmeric paste. The honey not only sweetens the paste but also adds its own antibacterial and immune-boosting properties.
5. Add 2 tablespoons of coconut oil to the mixture. The coconut oil enhances the absorption of curcumin in the body and adds a healthy fat source, which is beneficial for the immune system.
6. Mix in 1 1/2 teaspoons of black pepper. The piperine in black pepper significantly boosts the bioavailability of curcumin, making the turmeric more effective.
7. Once all the ingredients are well combined, transfer the turmeric immune paste into a clean, dry glass jar with a tight-fitting lid.

Variations

- For an extra immune boost, add 1 teaspoon of ground cinnamon or ground ginger to the paste. Both spices offer additional anti-inflammatory and antimicrobial benefits.

- If you prefer a vegan version, substitute honey with maple syrup to maintain the natural sweetness and health benefits.

- For those sensitive to coconut oil, olive oil can be used as a substitute, providing a different but still healthy fat source.

Storage tips

Store the Turmeric Immune Paste in the refrigerator in an airtight glass jar. The paste can be kept for up to 2-3 weeks. For longer storage, the paste can be frozen in an ice cube tray and then transferred to a freezer-safe bag or container for easy portioning.

Tips for allergens

Individuals with allergies to honey can use maple syrup as a sweetener alternative. For those with a black pepper allergy, it can be omitted; however, this may reduce the bioavailability of curcumin from the turmeric. Always ensure that all ingredients are certified organic to avoid potential contaminants and allergens.

20.4: Winter Cold and Flu Solutions

Fire Cider Remedy

Beneficial effects

Fire Cider Remedy is a traditional folk tonic revered for its ability to boost immune function, ward off colds and flu, stimulate digestion, and increase circulation. This spicy, sour, and slightly sweet concoction combines the powerful antimicrobial and antioxidant properties of ingredients like garlic, ginger, and apple cider vinegar. It's particularly beneficial during the winter months when the risk of infections is higher. Regular consumption can help to clear sinus congestion, warm the body, and support overall health.

Portions

Makes about 32 ounces

Preparation time

20 minutes

Cooking time

0 minutes (4-6 weeks for infusion)

Ingredients

- 1/2 cup fresh grated ginger root

- 1/2 cup fresh grated horseradish root

- 1 medium onion, chopped

- 10 cloves of garlic, minced

- 2 jalapeno peppers, chopped

- Zest and juice from 1 lemon

- Zest and juice from 1 orange

- 1/4 teaspoon cayenne pepper

- 1 tablespoon turmeric powder or 2 tablespoons fresh turmeric root, grated

- 1/4 cup fresh rosemary leaves

- 1/4 cup fresh thyme leaves

- 4 cups raw apple cider vinegar

- 1/4 cup raw honey, or to taste

Instructions

1. In a large glass jar, combine ginger, horseradish, onion, garlic, jalapeno peppers, lemon zest and juice, orange zest and juice, cayenne pepper, turmeric, rosemary, and thyme.
2. Pour apple cider vinegar over the ingredients until completely submerged. If necessary, use a piece of parchment paper under the lid to avoid corrosion from the vinegar.
3. Seal the jar tightly and shake well to mix all the ingredients.
4. Store the jar in a cool, dark place for 4-6 weeks, shaking daily to help the infusion process.
5. After 4-6 weeks, strain the mixture through a fine mesh strainer or cheesecloth, pressing or squeezing the solids to extract as much liquid as possible.
6. Stir in raw honey to the strained liquid, adjusting the amount according to your sweetness preference.
7. Transfer the finished Fire Cider into clean, sterilized bottles.

Variations

- Add a few sprigs of fresh dill or a few tablespoons of dried elderberries for additional immune support.

- For a sweeter version, increase the amount of honey, or add a few chopped apples to the initial mixture before infusing.

- Substitute one of the jalapeno peppers with a habanero for extra heat, if desired.

Storage tips

Store the Fire Cider Remedy in a cool, dark place. It will keep for up to 12 months if properly sealed. Refrigeration is not necessary but can be used if preferred, especially after opening.

Tips for allergens

For those with honey allergies, substitute with maple syrup to maintain the natural sweetness without the allergenic concern. If sensitive to any of the spicy ingredients, adjust the quantities or omit as necessary, keeping in mind this may alter the traditional flavor and potency of the remedy.

Ginger-Honey Cough Syrup Remedy

Beneficial effects

Ginger-Honey Cough Syrup Remedy utilizes the natural expectorant properties of ginger to loosen and expel mucus from the respiratory tract, easing coughs. Honey acts as a natural cough suppressant, soothing the throat and reducing cough severity. Together, they form a powerful duo that not only alleviates symptoms but also provides antibacterial benefits, potentially reducing the duration of a cold.

Portions

Makes about 1 cup

Preparation time

5 minutes

Cooking time

20 minutes

Ingredients

- 1/4 cup fresh ginger root, peeled and finely chopped

- 1 cup water

- 1/3 cup raw, organic honey

- Juice of 1/2 lemon (optional, for added vitamin C and flavor)

Instructions

1. Combine 1/4 cup of finely chopped fresh ginger root with 1 cup of water in a small saucepan.
2. Bring the mixture to a boil over medium-high heat, then reduce the heat to low and simmer for 20 minutes. The simmering process allows the ginger to infuse the water, extracting its beneficial compounds.
3. After simmering, strain the ginger pieces from the liquid using a fine mesh strainer, pressing the ginger to extract as much liquid as possible. Discard the ginger solids.
4. While the ginger infusion is still warm (not hot), stir in 1/3 cup of raw, organic honey until it is completely dissolved. The warmth will help dissolve the honey without destroying its beneficial enzymes and properties.
5. If desired, add the juice of 1/2 lemon to the mixture for additional vitamin C, which can help boost the immune system, and for flavor.
6. Transfer the syrup to a clean, airtight glass jar or bottle for storage.

Variations

- For an extra immune boost, add a pinch of ground cinnamon or cayenne pepper to the syrup. Both spices are known for their anti-inflammatory and antioxidant properties.

- Substitute lemon juice with orange juice for a different citrus twist that still provides immune-boosting benefits.

- For those who prefer a thinner syrup, add an additional 1/4 cup of water during the simmering process.

Storage tips

Store the Ginger-Honey Cough Syrup in the refrigerator in an airtight container. It can be kept for up to 2 weeks. Shake well before each use as natural separation may occur.

Tips for allergens

Individuals with allergies to honey can substitute it with maple syrup, though the antibacterial properties may vary. For those allergic to citrus, omit the lemon juice to avoid any adverse reactions.

Chapter 21: Practical Tips and Add-Ons

21.1: Batch-Making Remedies

To start batch-making remedies for prolonged use, it's essential to understand the process of scaling up from small, individual preparations to larger quantities. This ensures not only a steady supply of remedies but also consistency in strength and effectiveness. Begin by selecting a recipe that has proven effective on a smaller scale, ensuring its components scale up appropriately. Some ingredients may require adjustments due to their potency when increased in volume.

Selecting Containers and Labels: For storage, choose glass jars or bottles with tight-fitting lids to protect the contents from air and light. Amber or blue glass is preferable for light-sensitive preparations. Always label each container with the remedy name, date of production, and expiry date. This practice is crucial for tracking the potency and safety of the remedy over time.

Calculating Ingredients: When scaling up, use a digital scale for precise measurements, especially for dry herbs and powders. Liquid ingredients can be measured with graduated cylinders or measuring cups designed for liquid volumes. Ensure all measurements are converted correctly when scaling, maintaining the ratio of herbs to solvents.

Mixing Techniques: For large batches, a clean, dry, and spacious mixing bowl or pot is necessary. Mix dry ingredients thoroughly before adding any liquids. When preparing tinctures or oil infusions, stir the mixture gently to ensure even distribution of the herbs. For water-based preparations like teas or decoctions, a large stainless steel pot is ideal for simmering ingredients.

Heating and Simmering: When recipes require heating, use a controlled heat source that allows for consistent simmering. A double boiler setup is beneficial for gently heating oil infusions without direct contact with the heat source, minimizing the risk of overheating. For decoctions, maintain a gentle simmer and cover the pot to prevent the loss of volatile compounds.

Straining and Bottling: After the preparation has steeped or simmered for the required time, strain the mixture using a fine mesh strainer or cheesecloth. For large volumes, a press may be necessary to efficiently extract liquids from the plant material. Transfer the strained liquid into prepared containers using a funnel to avoid spillage. Ensure the containers are clean and dry to prevent contamination.

Storage Conditions: Store the remedies in a cool, dark place to preserve their potency. Some preparations may require refrigeration, especially those without preservatives or those prone to spoilage. Check the remedies periodically for signs of spoilage, such as off-odors, discoloration, or mold growth.

Batch Testing: Before using the remedy extensively, test a small amount to confirm its effectiveness and detect any adverse reactions. This step is particularly important when introducing new ingredients or when scaling up significantly from the original recipe.

Record Keeping: Maintain detailed records of each batch, including the source and quality of ingredients, exact measurements, preparation methods, and any variations from the original recipe. This documentation is invaluable for replicating successful batches and troubleshooting any issues.

By following these detailed steps, practitioners can efficiently produce large quantities of natural remedies, ensuring a reliable supply for extended use. This approach not only maximizes the benefits of herbal preparations but also supports a sustainable practice of natural wellness.

21.2. Creating Custom Blends

Custom Herbal Tea Blend

Beneficial effects

The Custom Herbal Tea Blend is designed to support immune health, promote relaxation, and aid digestion. This blend combines the soothing properties of chamomile, the immune-boosting benefits of echinacea, and the digestive aid of peppermint. Chamomile is known for its calming effects, making it ideal for stress relief and improved sleep. Echinacea enhances the body's immune response, helping to ward off colds and flu. Peppermint soothes the stomach and improves digestion, making this tea blend a versatile addition to your wellness routine.

Portions

Makes about 4 cups

Preparation time

10 minutes

Cooking time

5 minutes

Ingredients

- 2 tablespoons dried chamomile flowers

- 1 tablespoon dried echinacea leaves

- 1 tablespoon dried peppermint leaves

- 4 cups boiling water

- Honey or lemon to taste (optional)

Instructions

1. In a large teapot or heat-resistant pitcher, combine 2 tablespoons of dried chamomile flowers, 1 tablespoon of dried echinacea leaves, and 1 tablespoon of dried peppermint leaves.
2. Pour 4 cups of boiling water over the herbs. Cover the teapot or pitcher with a lid or a plate to keep the steam in, which aids in the infusion process.
3. Allow the tea to steep for 5 minutes. Steeping for this duration ensures that the medicinal qualities of the herbs are well extracted into the water.
4. Strain the tea through a fine mesh sieve into four cups, pressing against the herbs with a spoon to extract as much liquid and beneficial properties as possible.
5. If desired, sweeten each cup with honey or add a squeeze of lemon for flavor. Honey provides additional soothing properties for the throat, while lemon adds a refreshing tang and can aid in digestion.

Variations

- For a calming nighttime tea, add a teaspoon of dried lavender to the blend. Lavender's relaxing properties can further enhance the stress-relieving benefits of chamomile.

- Incorporate a slice of fresh ginger to the tea while it steeps for added digestive support and a warming effect.

- To make a cold soothing tea, allow the tea to cool completely, then refrigerate. Serve over ice for a refreshing digestive aid during warmer months.

Storage tips

The tea is best enjoyed fresh, but any leftovers can be stored in the refrigerator for up to 24 hours. Reheat gently or enjoy cold.

Tips for allergens

For those with sensitivities to honey, a simple alternative is to sweeten the tea with maple syrup or to enjoy it unsweetened. Ensure that individuals with pollen allergies are aware of the chamomile content, as chamomile is related to ragweed and may trigger allergies in susceptible individuals.

Spicy Immunity Boosting Blend

Beneficial effects

The Spicy Immunity Boosting Blend is crafted to enhance the body's natural defenses against common colds, flu, and other respiratory infections. Ingredients like ginger and turmeric offer potent anti-inflammatory and antioxidant properties, aiding in reducing inflammation and bolstering the immune system. Cayenne pepper, with its high content of capsaicin, helps in improving blood circulation and relieving congestion. Together, these spices create a powerful tonic that not only supports immune function but also provides a warming sensation, ideal for chilly days or when feeling under the weather.

Portions

Makes about 2 cups

Preparation time

15 minutes

Ingredients

- 1/4 cup dried ginger powder

- 1/4 cup turmeric powder

- 2 tablespoons cayenne pepper

- 1/2 cup raw, organic honey

- 2 tablespoons apple cider vinegar

- 4 cups boiling water

- Juice of 1 lemon

Instructions

1. In a large heat-resistant mixing bowl, combine 1/4 cup of dried ginger powder, 1/4 cup of turmeric powder, and 2 tablespoons of cayenne pepper.
2. Pour 4 cups of boiling water over the spice mixture. Stir well to ensure all the spices are fully dissolved in the water.
3. Allow the mixture to steep for 10 minutes, covering the bowl with a plate or lid to retain heat and steam.
4. After steeping, strain the mixture through a fine mesh sieve into a clean pitcher or jar, pressing on the solids to extract as much liquid as possible.
5. While the liquid is still warm, stir in 1/2 cup of raw, organic honey and 2 tablespoons of apple cider vinegar until fully dissolved. The honey adds a natural sweetness that balances the spiciness, while the vinegar contributes to the tonic's immune-boosting properties.
6. Squeeze the juice of 1 lemon into the blend and stir well. Lemon juice adds a refreshing tang and provides an additional boost of vitamin C.
7. Serve the blend warm, or allow it to cool and store in the refrigerator for a chilled beverage.

Variations

- For a herbal twist, add a handful of fresh mint leaves or echinacea during the steeping process to enhance the blend's immune-boosting capabilities.

- Incorporate a teaspoon of black pepper to increase the bioavailability of turmeric's curcumin, maximizing its health benefits.

- Replace honey with maple syrup for a vegan-friendly sweetener option that complements the spicy flavors.

Storage tips

Store the Spicy Immunity Boosting Blend in an airtight glass container in the refrigerator for up to one week. Gently reheat before serving or enjoy cold, depending on personal preference.

Tips for allergens

For those with allergies to honey, maple syrup serves as an excellent alternative, offering a similar texture and natural sweetness. If sensitive to cayenne pepper, reduce the amount used or substitute with a milder spice like paprika to maintain the blend's warming qualities without the intense heat.

Calming Sleep Aid Blend

Beneficial effects

The Calming Sleep Aid Blend is crafted to naturally promote relaxation and improve sleep quality. Lavender, known for its soothing and calming properties, helps to ease the mind and reduce anxiety, making it easier to fall asleep. Chamomile enhances these effects by further relaxing the muscles and acting as a gentle sedative. Together, they create a powerful duo that can help individuals struggling with insomnia or restless nights to achieve a deeper, more restorative sleep.

Ingredients

- 2 tablespoons dried lavender flowers

- 2 tablespoons dried chamomile flowers

- 1 cup boiling water

- 1 teaspoon honey (optional)

- 1/4 teaspoon ground cinnamon (optional for added warmth and comfort)

Instructions

1. Boil 1 cup of water in a kettle or on the stove.
2. Place 2 tablespoons of dried lavender flowers and 2 tablespoons of dried chamomile flowers in a tea infuser or directly into a teapot.
3. Once the water reaches a rolling boil, pour it over the lavender and chamomile flowers in the teapot.
4. Cover the teapot with a lid and allow the blend to steep for 5-7 minutes. The steeping time allows the herbs to release their essential oils and active compounds into the water, maximizing the calming effects.
5. After steeping, remove the tea infuser or strain the blend to remove the loose flowers.
6. If desired, stir in 1 teaspoon of honey to sweeten the blend. The honey can add a comforting sweetness that may enhance the calming experience.
7. For added warmth and comfort, sprinkle 1/4 teaspoon of ground cinnamon into the tea and stir well.
8. Pour the prepared Calming Sleep Aid Blend into a cup and enjoy it warm before bedtime.

Variations

- For a citrus twist, add a few strips of orange peel to the blend before steeping. The citrus can provide a refreshing note and may further aid in relaxation.

- Incorporate a few leaves of fresh mint to the blend for a cooling effect that complements the floral notes of lavender and chamomile.

- Replace honey with maple syrup for a vegan-friendly sweetener that adds a rich, earthy flavor to the blend.

Storage tips

Store any leftover dried lavender and chamomile flowers in airtight containers in a cool, dark place to preserve their potency and freshness. The prepared Calming Sleep Aid Blend is best enjoyed fresh, but any leftovers can be stored in the refrigerator for up to 24 hours and gently reheated before consumption.

Tips for allergens

For individuals with allergies to honey, omitting the sweetener or substituting it with agave syrup can provide a similar sweetness without the allergenic concern. Ensure that the lavender and chamomile used are organic and free from pesticides to minimize the risk of allergic reactions.

Energizing Morning Blend

Beneficial effects

The Energizing Morning Blend is designed to kickstart your day with a burst of energy and focus. This blend combines the revitalizing properties of green tea, known for its high antioxidant content and ability to enhance mental alertness, with the adaptogenic benefits of ashwagandha, which helps the body manage stress and combat fatigue. The addition of lemon provides a refreshing flavor and vitamin C, supporting the immune system, while ginger adds a warming effect and aids digestion. This blend is perfect for those looking to naturally boost their energy levels and start the day on a positive note.

Portions

2 servings

Preparation time

5 minutes

Cooking time

10 minutes

Ingredients

- 2 teaspoons green tea leaves

- 1 teaspoon ashwagandha powder

- 1 inch fresh ginger root, peeled and thinly sliced

- Juice of 1 lemon

- 2 cups boiling water

- Honey to taste (optional)

Instructions

1. Boil 2 cups of water in a kettle or saucepan.
2. Place the green tea leaves, ashwagandha powder, and thinly sliced ginger root in a teapot or heat-resistant pitcher.
3. Pour the boiling water over the green tea, ashwagandha, and ginger in the teapot or pitcher.
4. Cover and allow the blend to steep for about 5-7 minutes. The steeping time allows for the extraction of the green tea's antioxidants, the ashwagandha's adaptogenic properties, and the ginger's warming and digestive benefits.
5. Strain the blend into two cups, removing the green tea leaves, ashwagandha powder, and ginger slices.
6. Squeeze the juice of 1 lemon evenly into the two cups, adding a refreshing and immune-boosting element to the blend.
7. If desired, sweeten with honey to taste, stirring well to ensure it dissolves completely.
8. Serve the Energizing Morning Blend warm, enjoying the invigorating and healthful start to your day.

Variations

- For an extra boost of energy, add a pinch of ground cinnamon or cayenne pepper to the blend before steeping. Both spices can help increase circulation and add a subtle spicy kick.

- Replace green tea with matcha powder for a more potent source of antioxidants and a richer flavor. Use 1/2 teaspoon of matcha powder per serving, whisking it into the boiling water before adding the other ingredients.

- For a cooler, refreshing version, allow the blend to cool and then serve over ice, making it a revitalizing cold beverage for warm mornings.

Storage tips

The Energizing Morning Blend is best enjoyed fresh. However, if you need to store any leftover blend, keep it in a sealed glass container in the refrigerator for up to 24 hours. Reheat gently on the stove or enjoy chilled.

Tips for allergens

Individuals with sensitivities to caffeine can reduce the amount of green tea or choose a decaffeinated variety. For those allergic to honey, substitute with maple syrup or enjoy the blend unsweetened to maintain its natural flavors and benefits.

Digestive Support Blend

Beneficial effects

Digestive Support Blend is a carefully crafted herbal formula designed to soothe digestive discomfort, promote healthy digestion, and support the overall function of the digestive system. This blend combines herbs known for their ability to relieve bloating, ease stomach cramps, and stimulate digestion, making it an excellent natural remedy for those experiencing digestive issues such as indigestion, gas, and irregular bowel movements. Regular use can help maintain a balanced digestive environment and enhance nutrient absorption.

Portions

Makes about 100 capsules or 1 cup of loose powder

Preparation time

20 minutes

Ingredients

- 1/2 cup dried peppermint leaves, finely ground

- 1/4 cup dried ginger root, finely ground

- 1/4 cup dried fennel seeds, finely ground

- 1 tablespoon dried licorice root, finely ground

- 1 tablespoon slippery elm bark, finely ground

Instructions

1. Begin by measuring each of the dried herbs: peppermint leaves, ginger root, fennel seeds, licorice root, and slippery elm bark. Ensure all ingredients are finely ground for consistency and easier blending.
2. In a clean, dry mixing bowl, combine the ground peppermint, ginger, fennel, licorice, and slippery elm bark. Mix thoroughly to ensure an even distribution of all ingredients.
3. Using a mortar and pestle or a small coffee grinder, further blend the mixture to achieve a fine, uniform powder. This step is crucial for the consistency of the capsules and the effectiveness of the blend.
4. If making capsules, carefully spoon the powder into capsule shells using a capsule filling machine or a small spoon. Follow the manufacturer's instructions for your capsule machine to ensure the capsules are properly filled and sealed.
5. If using as a loose powder, transfer the final blend into a clean, dry glass jar with a tight-fitting lid. Label the jar with the contents and date.

Variations

- For added digestive support, include 1 teaspoon of ground cardamom to the blend. Cardamom can help reduce stomach acidity and relieve nausea.

- If capsules are not preferred, this blend can be made into a tea. Simply mix 1 teaspoon of the powder with 8 ounces of boiling water, steep for 10 minutes, and strain before drinking.

- For those sensitive to licorice root, it can be omitted or replaced with an equal amount of marshmallow root, which also provides soothing mucilage beneficial for the digestive tract.

Storage tips

Store the Digestive Support Blend in a cool, dry place, away from direct sunlight. Capsules should be kept in a sealed container, and loose powder should be stored in an airtight glass jar. Both forms will maintain potency for up to 6 months when stored properly.

Tips for allergens

For individuals with allergies to any of the herbs listed, substitute with another herb that has similar digestive benefits, such as chamomile for its soothing properties, ensuring no adverse reactions. Always consult with a healthcare provider before starting any new herbal regimen, especially if you have existing health conditions or are taking medications.

21.3. Herbal Storage and Shelf Life

When it comes to maximizing the efficacy of your herbal remedies through proper storage, understanding the nuances of how different herbs interact with various storage conditions is paramount. Each herb has its unique requirements for maintaining potency, and several factors come into play, including humidity, temperature, light, and air exposure. Here, we delve into the specifics of preserving your herbal collection to ensure longevity and effectiveness.

Humidity Control: Herbs need to be stored in a dry environment to prevent mold and bacterial growth. Silica gel packets can be an effective solution for absorbing excess moisture in storage containers. Alternatively, storing herbs in an area with a dehumidifier can help maintain an optimal dry environment. Ensure that your storage area maintains a relative humidity level below 60% to safeguard the herbs from moisture-induced degradation.

Temperature Regulation: Heat can deteriorate the active compounds in herbs, leading to a loss of potency. Store your herbs in a cool place, ideally not exceeding 70°F (21°C). A cellar or a cool, dark pantry can provide the perfect environment. Avoid storing herbs near heat sources such as stoves, ovens, or direct sunlight, as these can accelerate the breakdown of essential oils and active ingredients.

Light Protection: Exposure to light, especially sunlight, can lead to the degradation of many herbs. Colored glass containers, such as amber or cobalt blue, offer protection against UV rays and preserve the quality of the herbs. If using clear glass or if colored containers are not available, storing the containers in a dark cupboard or covering them with a cloth can shield the herbs from harmful light exposure.

Airtight Containers: Oxygen exposure can oxidize herbs, affecting their flavor and medicinal properties. Using airtight containers is crucial for extending shelf life. Glass jars with rubber-sealed lids, vacuum-sealed bags, and metal tins with tight-fitting lids are all excellent choices. Ensure that the containers are completely dry before adding herbs to prevent moisture buildup.

Labeling and Organization: Properly labeling your herbs with the name, date of harvest or purchase, and expected shelf life can help you keep track of their potency over time. Organizing your herbs in a way that allows you to easily access and monitor them ensures that older herbs are used first, maintaining a cycle of freshness.

Specific Storage Techniques for Different Herb Forms:

- **Dried Herbs**: Store in airtight containers away from light and heat. They can last up to 1-3 years, depending on the herb.

- **Tinctures and Liquid Extracts**: Dark glass bottles are ideal. Store in cool, dark places, and they can last for several years.

- **Herbal Oils**: Refrigeration can extend the shelf life of infused oils. Use dark bottles to protect from light, and they can last up to a year.

- **Salves and Balms**: Store in cool places in tightly sealed containers. They typically last up to a year, depending on the ingredients used.

Regular Inspection: Periodically check your stored herbs for signs of spoilage, such as mold, pests, or unusual odors. Discard any herbs that show signs of degradation to ensure that your apothecary remains a source of potent, effective remedies.

By adhering to these detailed storage guidelines, you can significantly extend the life of your herbal remedies, ensuring that they retain their therapeutic properties for as long as possible. This attention to detail in storage practices underscores the importance of respecting the natural gifts these herbs offer, allowing you to harness their full potential for health and wellness.

Book 6: The Survivalist's Apothecary

Chapter 22: Emergency First Aid

In the realm of emergency first aid, the use of herbs for bleeding, infection, and pain relief is a vital skill set that can be life-saving in situations where conventional medical help is not immediately available. The knowledge of how to correctly identify, prepare, and apply herbal remedies is an indispensable part of any survivalist's toolkit. This section delves into the specifics of utilizing three powerful plants: yarrow, plantain leaf, and willow bark, each revered for their medicinal properties that can address common first aid situations such as bleeding, infection, and pain.

Yarrow (Achillea millefolium) is renowned for its ability to stop bleeding rapidly. To prepare a yarrow poultice, one must first gather fresh yarrow leaves and flowers. If fresh yarrow is not available, dried yarrow can be rehydrated with a small amount of boiling water. Crush or grind the plant material to release its active compounds. The resulting mash can be applied directly to the wound or wrapped in a clean cloth before being placed on the skin. The poultice should be secured with a bandage and left in place for up to an hour or until bleeding has significantly reduced. It's crucial to ensure that the yarrow used is correctly identified to avoid applying a potentially harmful plant.

Plantain Leaf (Plantago major) has been used for centuries as a natural remedy for infections and skin irritations. To create a plantain leaf salve, begin by finely chopping fresh plantain leaves. These should then be infused in a carrier oil, such as coconut or olive oil, over low heat for several hours to extract the active constituents. After straining out the plant material, beeswax can be melted into the oil at a ratio of approximately 1 ounce of beeswax per cup of oil to create a salve. This salve can be applied to cuts, scrapes, and other skin infections to promote healing and prevent infection. The key to an effective plantain leaf salve is the quality of the plant material and the careful preparation of the infusion.

Willow Bark (Salix spp.) contains salicin, a precursor to aspirin, making it an effective remedy for pain relief. To prepare a willow bark tincture, finely chop dried willow bark and place it in a jar, covering it with a high-proof alcohol such as vodka or brandy. The mixture should be allowed to steep for 4 to 6 weeks, shaking the jar daily. After steeping, the tincture can be strained and stored in a dark bottle. For pain relief, a dosage of 1-2 milliliters of the tincture can be taken up to three times a day. It is important to note that willow bark should not be used by individuals who are allergic to aspirin or who are taking blood-thinning medications.

Each of these herbal remedies offers a natural approach to addressing common first aid concerns. However, it is essential to remember that while these remedies can be effective, they are not substitutes for professional medical treatment in serious or life-threatening conditions. Proper identification and preparation of these herbs are crucial to their effectiveness and safety.

For natural antiseptics and coagulants, turning to the plant kingdom provides us with effective solutions that have been utilized throughout human history. **Yarrow (Achillea millefolium)**, beyond its ability to halt bleeding, also possesses antiseptic properties that can cleanse wounds and prevent infection. Creating a yarrow antiseptic wash involves steeping dried or fresh yarrow in boiling water for approximately 30 minutes. This potent infusion can then be cooled and applied to wounds with a clean cloth or used to rinse affected areas, offering a dual action of stopping bleeding and cleansing.

Plantain Poultice (Plantago major), much like the salve, can be used for its wound-healing properties. For immediate use in the field, fresh plantain leaves can be chewed or crushed and applied directly to wounds. This method quickly releases the plant's natural antimicrobial and anti-inflammatory compounds, providing a protective barrier against pathogens and soothing injured skin. The simplicity of this preparation makes it an invaluable technique for emergency situations where time and resources may be limited.

Comfrey (Symphytum officinale), known for its remarkable healing properties, especially in healing broken bones and sprains, can also be used to create a **Comfrey Coagulation Balm**. To make this, comfrey leaves should be infused in a carrier oil, similar to the plantain leaf salve preparation. After straining, beeswax is added to thicken the mixture. Applied to bruises or sprained areas, comfrey balm supports the healing of tissues and can be an essential part of a natural first aid kit. However, due to its powerful active compounds, comfrey should be used with caution and never applied to open wounds or broken skin.

Understanding the proper application and potential risks of these natural remedies is crucial. While **yarrow** and **plantain** offer broad-spectrum benefits for various first aid scenarios, **comfrey** should be reserved for specific conditions under the guidance of a knowledgeable herbalist, especially considering its potent effects and the caution required in its use.

Incorporating these plants into a survivalist's apothecary not only empowers one to manage emergencies with natural solutions but also deepens the connection to the natural world. Mastery of these remedies enhances resilience, self-reliance, and the ability to provide care with the gifts of the earth. As with any herbal remedy, the effectiveness is greatly influenced by the quality of the herbs, the precision of preparation, and the understanding of their appropriate use. Therefore, continuous learning, practice, and respect for nature's potency are paramount in the effective application of these ancient healing practices.

22.1: Herbs for Bleeding, Infection, and Pain Relief

Yarrow Poultice for Bleeding

Beneficial effects

Yarrow Poultice for Bleeding harnesses the powerful astringent properties of yarrow, an herb known for its ability to stop bleeding, reduce inflammation, and promote wound healing. Yarrow contains compounds that can quickly coagulate blood, making it an invaluable remedy for cuts, abrasions, and deeper wounds. Its natural antiseptic qualities also help prevent infection, supporting the body's healing process.

Portions

Enough for 1-2 applications, depending on wound size

Preparation time

5 minutes

Ingredients

- 2 tablespoons dried yarrow leaves and flowers

- Enough hot water to form a paste

- Clean gauze or cloth for application

Instructions

1. Place 2 tablespoons of dried yarrow leaves and flowers in a small bowl.
2. Slowly add hot water to the yarrow, a few drops at a time, while stirring continuously to form a thick paste. The consistency should be spreadable but not runny, to ensure it adheres to the wound area without dripping.
3. Allow the yarrow paste to cool slightly until it is warm but not hot to the touch.
4. While the paste cools, gently clean the wound with mild soap and water, patting dry with a clean towel.
5. Apply a generous layer of the yarrow paste directly onto the cleaned wound.
6. Cover the paste with a piece of clean gauze or cloth, securing it in place with medical tape or a bandage.
7. Leave the poultice on the wound for up to 30 minutes. Monitor the wound for any signs of increased irritation or allergic reaction during this time.
8. Carefully remove the gauze or cloth and rinse the area with cool water.
9. Apply a fresh bandage if necessary.

Variations

- For enhanced healing properties, mix the yarrow with a teaspoon of honey before adding water. Honey provides additional antibacterial benefits and can help keep the wound moist for optimal healing.

- If fresh yarrow is available, you can chop the leaves and flowers finely and use them directly without adding water to form a fresh poultice.

Storage tips

Store unused dried yarrow in an airtight container in a cool, dark place to maintain its potency. Once water is added to make a paste, it is best used immediately, as the poultice does not store well and could harbor bacteria if kept for later use.

Tips for allergens

Individuals with sensitivity to plants in the Asteraceae family, such as chamomile or ragweed, may also react to yarrow. Always perform a patch test on a small area of skin away from the wound to check for any adverse reaction before applying the poultice widely.

Scientific references

- "The effect of Achillea millefolium (Yarrow) on wound healing; a systematic review" in the Journal of Ethnopharmacology. This review highlights the wound-healing properties of yarrow, supporting its traditional use in stopping bleeding and promoting tissue repair.

Plantain Leaf Salve for Infection

Beneficial effects

Plantain Leaf Salve for Infection harnesses the natural antibacterial and anti-inflammatory properties of plantain leaves, making it an effective remedy for treating skin infections, cuts, and wounds. Plantain leaves contain allantoin, which promotes skin regeneration, reduces inflammation, and accelerates the healing process. This salve can be used to soothe insect bites, rashes, and minor burns, providing a protective barrier that supports the body's natural healing mechanisms.

Portions

Makes about 4 ounces

Preparation time

15 minutes

Cooking time

1 hour

Ingredients

- 1/2 cup dried plantain leaves, finely chopped or ground

- 1 cup olive oil or coconut oil

- 1/4 cup beeswax pellets

- 10 drops lavender essential oil (for additional antimicrobial and soothing properties)

- 5 drops tea tree essential oil (for enhanced antibacterial benefits)

Instructions

1. Combine 1/2 cup of dried plantain leaves with 1 cup of olive oil or coconut oil in a double boiler. Heat the mixture over low heat for 1 hour, allowing the plantain leaves to infuse their properties into the oil. Stir occasionally to ensure even heating.
2. After 1 hour, carefully strain the oil through a cheesecloth or fine mesh strainer into a clean bowl, removing all plant material. Press the plantain leaves to extract as much oil as possible.
3. Return the strained oil to the double boiler and add 1/4 cup of beeswax pellets. Heat the mixture over low heat, stirring constantly, until the beeswax is completely melted and combined with the oil.
4. Remove the mixture from heat and let it cool slightly for about 2-3 minutes.
5. Stir in 10 drops of lavender essential oil and 5 drops of tea tree essential oil into the slightly cooled mixture. These essential oils add additional antimicrobial and soothing properties to the salve.
6. Carefully pour the warm salve into clean, dry tins or glass jars. Allow the salve to cool and solidify at room temperature.
7. Once solidified, seal the containers with lids to preserve the salve.

Variations

- For a vegan version, substitute beeswax pellets with the same amount of candelilla wax.

- Add a teaspoon of vitamin E oil to the mixture after removing it from heat to act as a natural preservative and skin conditioner.

- For extra soothing properties, include a tablespoon of calendula oil in the oil infusion step.

Storage tips

Store the Plantain Leaf Salve in a cool, dry place, away from direct sunlight. If stored properly in an airtight container, the salve can last for up to 1 year. For best results, keep it in a cool environment to maintain its consistency.

Tips for allergens

Individuals with sensitivities to lavender or tea tree oil can reduce the amount used or omit these oils entirely. Substitute with chamomile essential oil for a milder, yet still effective, antimicrobial alternative. Always perform a patch test on a small area of skin before applying the salve extensively, especially if you have sensitive skin or known allergies.

Willow Bark Pain Relief Tincture

Beneficial effects

Willow Bark Pain Relief Tincture harnesses the natural pain-relieving properties of willow bark, known for its active compound salicin, which the body converts into salicylic acid, providing relief similar to aspirin without the synthetic additives. This tincture can help alleviate headaches, reduce inflammation, and soothe arthritic and lower back pain, making it a valuable natural remedy for those seeking alternatives to over-the-counter pain medications.

Portions

Makes about 1 pint

Preparation time

15 minutes

Cooking time

24 hours for infusion

Ingredients

- 1 cup dried willow bark, finely chopped

- 2 cups 100-proof vodka

Instructions

1. Place 1 cup of finely chopped dried willow bark into a clean, dry glass jar.
2. Pour 2 cups of 100-proof vodka over the willow bark, ensuring the bark is completely submerged. The alcohol extracts the salicin from the willow bark, turning it into a potent tincture.
3. Seal the jar tightly with a lid. Shake the jar vigorously to mix the willow bark with the vodka thoroughly.
4. Label the jar with the date and contents. Store the jar in a cool, dark place, such as a cupboard or a pantry, away from direct sunlight and temperature fluctuations.
5. Shake the jar once daily to facilitate the extraction process.
6. After 24 hours, strain the mixture through a fine mesh strainer or cheesecloth into another clean, dry jar, pressing or squeezing the willow bark to extract as much liquid as possible. Discard the willow bark solids.
7. Transfer the strained tincture into dark glass dropper bottles for easy dosage and storage. Label the bottles with the date and contents.

Variations

- For added anti-inflammatory benefits, include a teaspoon of dried ginger root to the willow bark during the infusion process. Ginger enhances the tincture's pain-relieving properties and adds a warming effect.

- To create a more complex pain relief tincture, combine willow bark with other herbs known for their analgesic properties, such as turmeric or St. John's Wort, following the same proportions and infusion time.

Storage tips

Store the Willow Bark Pain Relief Tincture in a cool, dark place, ideally in a cabinet or a drawer, to protect it from light degradation. If stored properly, the tincture can last for up to 5 years, maintaining its potency and effectiveness.

Tips for allergens

For individuals sensitive to alcohol, the tincture can be evaporated by adding the required dose to hot water or tea, allowing the alcohol to evaporate before consumption. Always consult with a healthcare provider before using willow bark, especially for those with allergies to aspirin or other salicylates.

22.2: Natural Antiseptics and Coagulants

Yarrow Antiseptic Wash

Beneficial effects

Yarrow Antiseptic Wash utilizes the potent antiseptic and hemostatic properties of yarrow, making it an excellent natural remedy for cleaning wounds and promoting healing. Yarrow (Achillea millefolium) has been used traditionally for its ability to stop bleeding, reduce inflammation, and kill bacteria. This wash can be applied to cuts, scrapes, and abrasions to prevent infection and support the body's natural healing processes.

Ingredients

- 1/4 cup dried yarrow flowers and leaves

- 2 cups boiling water

- 1 teaspoon salt (to enhance antiseptic quality)

Instructions

1. Boil 2 cups of water in a kettle or pot.
2. Place 1/4 cup of dried yarrow flowers and leaves in a heat-resistant bowl or jar.
3. Pour the boiling water over the yarrow, ensuring the plant material is fully submerged.
4. Add 1 teaspoon of salt to the mixture. Salt, a natural antiseptic, will help to disinfect the wound while enhancing the medicinal properties of the yarrow.
5. Cover the bowl or jar with a lid or plate and let the yarrow steep for 30 minutes. This steeping time allows the water to extract the yarrow's active compounds.
6. After 30 minutes, strain the yarrow infusion through a fine mesh sieve or cheesecloth into another clean container, pressing on the plant material to extract as much liquid as possible. Discard the used yarrow.
7. Allow the yarrow antiseptic wash to cool to room temperature before use.

Variations

- For added antimicrobial properties, include a tablespoon of honey to the cooled yarrow wash. Honey is known for its wound-healing and antibacterial effects.

- To make a stronger infusion, add a tablespoon of dried calendula flowers to the yarrow before pouring boiling water. Calendula enhances the wash's ability to fight infection and promote skin repair.

- For those sensitive to salt on open wounds, omit the salt and instead add a few drops of lavender essential oil to the cooled wash for its soothing and antimicrobial benefits.

Storage tips

Store the cooled yarrow antiseptic wash in a clean, airtight glass container in the refrigerator for up to one week. Label the container with the date it was made to ensure freshness. For longer-term storage, freeze the wash in ice cube trays and thaw as needed for use.

Tips for allergens

Individuals with allergies to plants in the Asteraceae family, such as chamomile or ragweed, may also react to yarrow. Conduct a patch test on an unaffected area of skin before applying the wash to wounds. If using honey, ensure it is pure and free from additives that may cause allergic reactions.

Plantain Poultice for Wounds

Beneficial effects

Plantain Poultice for Wounds utilizes the natural healing properties of plantain leaves, which are known for their antibacterial, anti-inflammatory, and wound-healing capabilities. The active compounds in plantain leaves, such as allantoin, promote cell growth and tissue repair, making this poultice an effective natural remedy for cuts, scrapes, and other skin injuries. Additionally, the astringent properties of plantain help to stop bleeding and reduce swelling, providing a protective barrier against infection and speeding up the healing process.

Portions

Enough for 2-3 applications

Preparation time

10 minutes

Ingredients

- 1/2 cup fresh plantain leaves, washed and patted dry

- 2-4 tablespoons of water (as needed to form a paste)

- Clean cloth or gauze for application

Instructions

1. Begin by finely chopping or crushing 1/2 cup of fresh plantain leaves using a mortar and pestle or a food processor to release their natural juices and active compounds.
2. Gradually add 2-4 tablespoons of water to the crushed plantain leaves, mixing continuously until a thick paste is formed. The amount of water needed may vary depending on the moisture content of the leaves.
3. Spread a generous amount of the plantain paste directly onto the clean cloth or gauze.
4. Apply the cloth or gauze with the plantain paste to the affected area, ensuring the wound is completely covered.
5. Secure the poultice in place with medical tape or a bandage, being careful not to apply too tightly.
6. Leave the poultice on the wound for up to 1 hour, monitoring for any signs of irritation or discomfort.
7. Gently remove the poultice and wash the area with clean, cool water.
8. Apply a fresh poultice 2-3 times daily as needed for continued wound care and healing.

Variations

- For enhanced antimicrobial properties, add 1 teaspoon of finely ground turmeric to the plantain paste before application. Turmeric's curcumin content adds additional anti-inflammatory and antibacterial benefits.

- To soothe particularly painful wounds, incorporate 1 tablespoon of aloe vera gel into the plantain paste for its cooling and healing effects.

Storage tips

Fresh plantain leaves should be used immediately for the highest potency, but any unused leaves can be stored in the refrigerator, wrapped in a damp paper towel and placed in a plastic bag, for up to 1 week. The prepared plantain paste should be used immediately and is not suitable for storage due to the risk of bacterial growth.

Tips for allergens

Individuals with sensitivities to plantain or other related plants should perform a patch test on a small, unaffected area of skin before applying the poultice to wounds. If irritation or an allergic reaction occurs, discontinue use immediately.

Comfrey Coagulation Balm

Beneficial effects

Comfrey Coagulation Balm utilizes the healing properties of comfrey, a plant renowned for its ability to speed up the healing of wounds, bruises, sprains, and broken bones. The active compound allantoin promotes cell regeneration, helping the skin to heal more quickly and effectively. This balm can be particularly beneficial in emergency first aid situations, providing a natural solution to help stop bleeding, reduce swelling, and protect the wound from infection.

Portions

Makes about 4 ounces

Preparation time

10 minutes

Cooking time

20 minutes

Ingredients

- 1/4 cup dried comfrey leaves

- 1/2 cup olive oil

- 2 tablespoons beeswax pellets

- 10 drops lavender essential oil

- 5 drops tea tree essential oil

Instructions

1. Begin by infusing the olive oil with dried comfrey leaves. Combine the comfrey leaves and olive oil in a double boiler and gently heat the mixture over low heat for 15 minutes, allowing the comfrey's beneficial properties to infuse into the oil.
2. After 15 minutes, carefully strain the oil through a cheesecloth or fine mesh strainer into a clean bowl, discarding the comfrey leaves. Ensure to press the leaves to extract as much oil as possible.
3. Return the infused oil to the double boiler and add the beeswax pellets. Heat the mixture over low heat, stirring constantly, until the beeswax is completely melted and well incorporated with the oil.
4. Remove the mixture from the heat and allow it to cool for a few minutes, but not solidify.
5. Stir in the lavender and tea tree essential oils. These oils add additional antimicrobial and soothing properties to the balm, enhancing its effectiveness in wound care.
6. Pour the slightly cooled mixture into small tins or glass jars before it solidifies. Allow the balm to cool and set completely at room temperature.
7. Once solidified, seal the containers with lids to preserve the balm.

Variations

- For extra skin soothing properties, add a tablespoon of aloe vera gel to the mixture after removing it from the heat. Aloe vera can help soothe the skin and reduce inflammation.

- Substitute olive oil with coconut oil for a thicker consistency and additional antimicrobial benefits.

- For those sensitive to lavender or tea tree oil, substitute with chamomile essential oil for a gentler yet effective antimicrobial alternative.

Storage tips

Store the Comfrey Coagulation Balm in a cool, dry place, away from direct sunlight. If stored properly in an airtight container, the balm can last for up to 1 year. Keeping it in a refrigerator can extend its shelf life and provide a cooling effect upon application.

Tips for allergens

Individuals with sensitivities to beeswax can substitute it with candelilla wax for a vegan-friendly option. Always perform a patch test on a small area of skin before applying the balm extensively, especially if you have sensitive skin or known allergies to any of the ingredients.

Chapter 23: Survival Essentials

23.1: Edible Wild Plants for Food Security

Identifying and utilizing edible wild plants can significantly enhance food security in survival situations. Here's a detailed guide on several key plants to look for, their nutritional benefits, and how to safely prepare them.

Dandelion (Taraxacum officinale): Every part of the dandelion is edible. The leaves can be eaten raw in salads or cooked to reduce bitterness. Rich in vitamins A, C, and K, they also provide calcium, potassium, iron, and manganese. The roots can be dried, roasted, and ground into a coffee substitute. The flowers make a pleasant addition to salads or can be fermented to make dandelion wine.

Nettle (Urtica dioica): While nettles must be handled carefully due to their stinging hairs, once cooked, they lose their sting and offer a rich source of vitamins A, C, and K, as well as iron, potassium, manganese, and calcium. Nettles can be boiled and consumed like spinach or made into a nutritious tea.

Plantain (Plantago major): Not to be confused with the banana-like fruit, the plantain leaf is a common weed that can be found in many backyards. It's rich in calcium and vitamins A, C, and K. The leaves can be eaten raw in salads, cooked like greens, or used to make a healing tea.

Wild Garlic (Allium ursinum) and Wild Onion (Allium canadense): Both of these plants are identifiable by their distinctive smell. They can be used similarly to cultivated garlic and onions, adding flavor to dishes and providing vitamins C and B6, along with manganese, selenium, and antioxidants.

Purslane (Portulaca oleracea): This succulent plant is often found in gardens and cracks in sidewalks. It's a great source of Omega-3 fatty acids, vitamins E and C, and antioxidants. The leaves and stems can be eaten raw in salads or cooked like spinach.

Blackberries (Rubus spp.): Found in many regions, blackberries are not only delicious but also packed with vitamins C and K, fiber, and antioxidants. They can be eaten raw, made into jams or jellies, or baked into desserts.

Acorns (Quercus spp.): While acorns require processing to remove tannins, they are a valuable source of calories and nutrients, including protein, fats, and carbohydrates. They can be ground into flour after leaching out the bitterness with water.

Cattails (Typha spp.): Often found near water, the roots, shoots, and pollen of cattails are edible. The roots can be processed into flour, the shoots eaten raw or cooked, and the pollen used as a flour supplement.

Preparation and Safety Tips:

1. **Identification:** Always be 100% certain of a plant's identity before consuming it. Use field guides or consult with an expert if you are unsure.

2. **Testing for Edibility:** If you are unsure about a plant, you can perform a universal edibility test, which involves separating the plant into its parts, testing each part for skin irritation, then tasting small portions for adverse reactions over several hours.

3. **Harvesting:** Collect plants from areas free of pollution and away from roadsides. Avoid plants with signs of pesticide use.

4. **Preparation:** Properly clean and cook plants when necessary to eliminate potential pathogens. Some plants may have toxic parts or become more palatable and digestible when cooked.

Incorporating these wild edibles into your diet during survival situations can provide essential nutrients and a sustainable food source. However, the key to safely enjoying these natural bounties lies in thorough identification, understanding the proper preparation methods, and knowing the nutritional benefits of each plant. This knowledge not only enhances food security but also deepens our connection to the natural world, empowering us to take charge of our well-being with the resources provided by our environment.

23.2: Herbs for Water Purification

Solar Still Water Purification

Beneficial effects

Solar Still Water Purification leverages the natural process of evaporation and condensation to remove impurities and produce clean drinking water. This method is effective in emergency situations where access to clean water is limited, as it can purify water from various sources, including seawater, by removing salts, bacteria, and other pathogens. The distilled water produced through this method is safe for drinking, cooking, and personal hygiene, making it a vital survival skill in remote or disaster-stricken areas.

Portions

Produces approximately 1 quart (32 ounces) of purified water per day, depending on sunlight and weather conditions.

Preparation time

1 hour to set up

Cooking time

24 hours for optimal water production

Ingredients

- 1 large clear plastic sheet

- 1 small, clean container (such as a cup or bowl)

- 1 larger container or excavation (a hole in the ground)

- Non-toxic weights (stones or heavy objects)

- 1 length of tubing (optional, for easier water collection)

- Saltwater or contaminated water

- Vegetation (optional, for additional moisture)

Instructions

1. Dig a hole in the ground about 2 feet wide and 2 feet deep, where sunlight is abundant throughout the day.
2. Place the small container in the center of the hole. This container will collect the purified water.
3. If using, fill the bottom of the hole around the small container with saltwater, contaminated water, or vegetation. This will be the source of moisture that will evaporate and then condense into distilled water.
4. Cover the hole with the clear plastic sheet, ensuring it extends beyond the hole's edges by at least 1 foot on all sides.

5. Place non-toxic weights around the edges of the plastic sheet to secure it in place and create a seal.
6. Place a small weight, such as a stone, in the center of the plastic sheet directly above the small container. This will create a low point for condensed water to drip into the container.
7. If using, insert one end of the tubing into the small container, running it underneath the edge of the plastic sheet to the outside. This allows you to drink the collected water without dismantling the still.
8. Leave the solar still to operate for 24 hours. Water will evaporate from the ground or added sources, condense on the underside of the plastic, and drip into the small container.
9. After 24 hours, collect the purified water from the small container. If using tubing, you can drink directly from the tube.

Variations

- For increased water production, set up multiple solar stills in different locations to collect more water simultaneously.

- Add green vegetation inside the hole to increase moisture content and potentially increase water output. Ensure the vegetation is non-toxic and free from harmful chemicals or pesticides.

Storage tips

Collect purified water in clean, sterilized containers. Store in a cool, shaded area to prevent bacterial growth. If collected water is not immediately needed, it can be boiled or chemically treated before storage for added safety.

Tips for allergens

Ensure all materials used, especially the collection container and tubing, are made from food-grade, non-toxic materials to prevent contamination of the purified water.

Charcoal and Sand Filtration

Beneficial effects

Charcoal and Sand Filtration is a natural method to purify water, effectively removing impurities, bacteria, and harmful pathogens, making it safe for drinking. Activated charcoal absorbs toxins and contaminants due to its high adsorption capacity, while sand acts as a physical filter, trapping larger particles and sediments. This combination ensures a comprehensive purification process, providing a reliable source of clean water in emergency situations or when access to treated water is not available.

Portions

Enough for filtering approximately 5 gallons of water

Preparation time

30 minutes

Cooking time

No cooking required

Ingredients

- 1/2 gallon of fine sand

- 1/2 gallon of coarse sand

- 1/2 gallon of gravel

- 1/2 gallon of activated charcoal

- 5-gallon bucket with a hole drilled at the bottom

- Clean cloth or coffee filter

- Plastic tubing or spigot (optional)

Instructions

1. Begin by rinsing all the sand and gravel with clean water to remove any dust or impurities.
2. Place the clean cloth or coffee filter at the bottom of the 5-gallon bucket. This will prevent the filtration materials from escaping through the hole.
3. Layer the gravel in the bucket first. This bottom layer helps with drainage and supports the layers above it.
4. Add the coarse sand over the gravel layer, ensuring an even distribution. The coarse sand will trap larger particles and sediments.
5. Layer the fine sand on top of the coarse sand. The fine sand acts as a more precise filter, catching smaller impurities.
6. Finally, add the activated charcoal layer. The activated charcoal will remove toxins, bacteria, and some viruses from the water through adsorption.
7. If using, insert the plastic tubing or spigot into the hole drilled at the bottom of the bucket. Secure it tightly to prevent leaks. This will allow for easy access to the filtered water.
8. Pour unfiltered water slowly into the bucket, allowing it to percolate through the layers and exit through the bottom hole or spigot. Collect the filtered water in a clean container.
9. Replace the sand and charcoal periodically to maintain the effectiveness of the filtration system.

Variations

- For enhanced purification, add a layer of pebbles above the gravel to improve water distribution and prevent channeling.

- Incorporate a layer of crushed moringa seeds between the fine sand and activated charcoal for their natural coagulating and antimicrobial properties.

- For a portable version, construct a smaller filtration system using a 2-liter plastic bottle cut in half and layered similarly. This can be used for personal or small-scale water purification needs.

Storage tips

Store unused activated charcoal, sand, and gravel in airtight containers to keep them clean and dry until needed. Keep the filtration system covered when not in use to prevent contamination.

Tips for allergens

Ensure the activated charcoal is sourced from a reputable supplier and is free from any additives or chemicals that could leach into the water. For individuals sensitive to dust or particulates from sand and gravel, wear protective gear such as gloves and a mask during preparation.

Boiling and Cooling Method

Beneficial effects

The Boiling and Cooling Method for water purification is a simple yet effective technique to ensure water safety in emergency situations. Boiling kills bacteria, viruses, and parasites present in water, making it safe for drinking and cooking. This method does not require any special equipment beyond a heat source and a container, making it accessible in various scenarios. Cooling the water after boiling not only makes it safe to consume but also improves its taste.

Portions

Varies depending on water needs

Preparation time

5 minutes

Cooking time

1 minute of rolling boil, then allow time to cool

Ingredients

- Water

- Heat source (fire, stove, or electric kettle)

- Clean container or pot

Instructions

1. Fill a clean pot or container with water. If the water is cloudy or contains debris, pre-filter it using a clean cloth or coffee filter to remove any large particles.
2. Place the container on a heat source. If using an open fire, ensure the container is fire-safe and positioned securely over the flames.
3. Bring the water to a rolling boil. Once boiling, maintain the boil for at least one minute to effectively kill bacteria, viruses, and parasites. At altitudes above 6,562 feet (2,000 meters), extend the boiling time to three minutes, as water boils at a lower temperature due to decreased air pressure.

4. After boiling, remove the container from the heat source and allow the water to cool naturally. Do not cover the container, as this can reintroduce contaminants.

5. Once cooled, the water is ready for use. Transfer it to a clean, covered container for storage if not using immediately.

Variations

- To improve the taste of boiled water, pour it back and forth between two clean containers several times to re-oxygenate it.

- Add a pinch of salt to each quart or liter of boiled water to enhance its flavor.

- For additional purification, combine boiling with chemical treatment or filtration if chemicals or a filter are available.

Storage tips

Store cooled, boiled water in clean, sealed containers to prevent recontamination. Use within 1-2 days, or refrigerate to extend shelf life up to a week. Label containers with the date of boiling for reference.

Tips for allergens

This method is safe and does not introduce any allergens. However, ensure all containers and filters used in pre-filtering are clean and free from substances that could cause allergic reactions

.

Chapter 24: Building Your Portable Apothecary Kit

24.1: Essential Herbs for Any Scenario

Continuing from the foundational knowledge and practical skills imparted earlier, let's delve into the essential herbs that should be included in any survival apothecary kit. These herbs have been selected for their versatility, efficacy, and ease of use in a variety of scenarios, from first aid to chronic condition support.

1. **Lavender (Lavandula angustifolia)** - Known for its calming and antiseptic properties, lavender is indispensable for stress relief, sleep improvement, and treating cuts and burns. Its oil can be used to disinfect wounds and soothe insect bites.

2. **Peppermint (Mentha piperita)** - A versatile herb for digestive health, peppermint can alleviate symptoms of indigestion and nausea. Its cooling effect is also beneficial for relieving headaches when applied topically as an oil or consumed as a tea.

3. **Chamomile (Matricaria chamomilla)** - With its gentle sedative effects, chamomile is excellent for reducing anxiety, treating insomnia, and calming upset stomachs. It's also used topically to soothe skin irritations and inflammations.

4. **Echinacea (Echinacea spp.)** - This immune-boosting herb is crucial for preventing and treating colds, flu, and other infections. It can be taken as a tincture or tea at the first sign of illness to enhance the body's natural defense system.

5. **Ginger (Zingiber officinale)** - A powerful anti-inflammatory and digestive aid, ginger can be used to treat nausea, motion sickness, and digestive discomfort. It's also effective in reducing pain and inflammation when consumed as a tea or applied topically as a poultice.

6. **Calendula (Calendula officinalis)** - Known for its healing properties, calendula is used to treat cuts, wounds, and skin irritations. It can be applied as a salve, lotion, or used in a soothing bath.

7. **Yarrow (Achillea millefolium)** - Ideal for first aid, yarrow can stop bleeding, reduce fever, and act as an anti-inflammatory. It's also beneficial in treating colds and flu when consumed as a tea.

8. **Plantain (Plantago major)** - A must-have for skin care and wound healing, plantain leaves can be used fresh for immediate relief from insect bites, cuts, and rashes. It's also effective in drawing out splinters and infections.

9. **Willow Bark (Salix spp.)** - Known as nature's aspirin, willow bark can be used to relieve pain, inflammation, and fever. It's especially useful for headaches, menstrual cramps, and arthritis pain when taken as a tea or tincture.

10. **Goldenseal (Hydrastis canadensis)** - With its potent antimicrobial properties, goldenseal is effective against infections and digestive issues. It can be used as a tincture for its antiseptic properties or taken orally to support the immune system.

When assembling your portable apothecary kit, consider the form that best suits each herb. Dried herbs are lightweight and versatile, suitable for teas and infusions. Tinctures are concentrated and long-lasting, ideal for immune support and acute conditions. Salves and oils are perfect for topical applications, addressing skin issues and muscle pains.

For each herb, ensure you have detailed knowledge of its use, dosage, and any potential contraindications. Remember, the effectiveness of these herbs is maximized when they are of high quality and properly stored. Select organically grown herbs whenever possible to avoid contaminants and ensure potency.

Incorporating these ten essential herbs into your survival apothecary kit equips you with natural remedies for a wide range of health concerns, from acute injuries to chronic conditions. With these herbs at your disposal, you can confidently address many common health issues naturally and effectively, enhancing your resilience and well-being in any situation.

24.2: Creating Compact, Travel-Friendly Remedies

Creating compact, travel-friendly remedies requires thoughtful preparation and an understanding of how to condense essential herbal treatments into portable formats without sacrificing their potency. This process involves selecting the right form for each remedy, ensuring they are both effective and convenient to carry in any scenario, especially emergencies. Here are detailed steps and recommendations to achieve this:

Selecting the Right Containers: Opt for small, durable containers that protect the contents from light, air, and moisture. Amber glass bottles are ideal for tinctures and oils, as they block UV rays that can degrade the herbal properties. For salves and balms, metal tins with secure lids prevent leakage and are light enough to carry. Ensure all containers are clearly labeled with the remedy name, date of preparation, and dosage instructions.

Concentrating Remedies: When space is at a premium, concentrate your remedies. This means creating tinctures and extracts with a higher ratio of herbs to solvent, or reducing infusions and decoctions to a concentrated form that can be diluted with water when needed. For example, a strong tincture might be made using a 1:2 herb-to-alcohol ratio, and decoctions can be simmered down to a thick syrup.

Multi-Use Formulas: Develop remedies that serve multiple purposes to save space. A well-formulated herbal salve can treat cuts, scrapes, and burns while also serving as a moisturizer. A tincture blend featuring echinacea, goldenseal, and ginger can address immune support, digestive health, and inflammation simultaneously.

Drying Herbs for Tea Blends: Create your own tea blends by drying and mixing herbs. These can be stored in small, airtight bags or containers. To use, simply add hot water. This method is particularly useful for herbs that are beneficial in treating multiple conditions, such as peppermint for digestive issues and headaches.

Powdered Herbs and Capsules: For ease of transport and dosing, consider grinding herbs into a fine powder and filling capsules. This is especially useful for bitter herbs or those that require precise dosages. A capsule machine can streamline this process, allowing you to prepare numerous capsules at once.

Essential Oils: While not a direct substitute for all herbal remedies, essential oils are highly concentrated and can be used in small amounts to achieve therapeutic effects. A compact kit of selected essential oils can be versatile and space-saving for addressing issues like stress, sleep, and minor wounds.

Preparation of Portable First Aid Kits: Incorporate a variety of the above remedies into a small, organized kit that can be easily accessed in emergencies. This kit might include a few essential tinctures, a multi-purpose salve, a small selection of tea blends or capsules, and essential oils. Add a small booklet or cards with usage instructions for each remedy.

Storage and Maintenance: To ensure the longevity and efficacy of your portable remedies, store the kit in a cool, dark place and regularly check the contents for signs of degradation or expiration. Replace any remedies as needed to maintain the kit's readiness.

Customization for Personal Needs: Tailor your portable apothecary kit to meet personal or family health needs. Consider including remedies that address specific chronic conditions, allergies, or frequently encountered health issues.

By following these steps, you can create a comprehensive and compact apothecary kit that will serve you well in daily life and in emergency situations. This approach not only empowers you to take charge of your health with natural remedies but also ensures you're prepared to address a wide range of health concerns wherever you go.

Book 7: Advanced Apothecary Skills

Chapter 26. Growing and Harvesting Your Apothecary

26.1: Top 20 Must-Have Herbs

- **Lavender (Lavandula angustifolia)**: Known for its calming and relaxing properties, lavender is indispensable for stress relief and sleep support. Its antiseptic qualities also make it useful for treating cuts and burns.

- **Peppermint (Mentha piperita)**: This herb is a digestive aid, helping to soothe stomach issues and relieve headaches. Its refreshing scent can also enhance mental clarity and energy.

- **Chamomile (Matricaria chamomilla)**: Chamomile is a gentle herb, perfect for calming anxiety, soothing digestive problems, and promoting sleep. It's particularly beneficial for children, making it a must-have in any family apothecary.

- **Echinacea (Echinacea spp.)**: Known for its immune-boosting properties, Echinacea is crucial for warding off colds and flu. It can also be applied topically to heal wounds and skin irritations.

- **Ginger (Zingiber officinale)**: A powerful anti-inflammatory and digestive aid, ginger can relieve nausea, motion sickness, and stomach discomfort. It also supports immune function and can warm the body in cold weather.

- **Turmeric (Curcuma longa)**: With its strong anti-inflammatory properties, turmeric is essential for managing pain and inflammation. It's also beneficial for skin health and can be used in cooking for added health benefits.

- **Garlic (Allium sativum)**: A natural antibiotic, garlic is essential for fighting infections. It also supports cardiovascular health and has antiviral and antifungal properties.

- **Calendula (Calendula officinalis)**: Calendula is a skin-healing powerhouse, useful for treating cuts, burns, and skin irritations. Its anti-inflammatory properties make it beneficial for digestive health as well.

- **Lemon Balm (Melissa officinalis)**: This herb is a mood lifter and natural sedative, making it perfect for reducing stress and anxiety. It can also help with digestive issues and is effective in treating cold sores.

- **Rosemary (Rosmarinus officinalis)**: Rosemary supports cognitive function and memory, making it a great herb for mental clarity. It also has pain-relieving properties and can aid in digestion.

- **Thyme (Thymus vulgaris)**: With its strong antimicrobial properties, thyme is excellent for treating coughs, colds, and throat infections. It's also a powerful antiseptic for cleaning wounds.

- **Sage (Salvia officinalis)**: Sage is beneficial for oral health, sore throat relief, and can alleviate digestive problems. It's also known for its cognitive-enhancing effects.

- **Basil (Ocimum basilicum)**: Basil is not just a culinary herb; it has anti-inflammatory and antibacterial properties, making it useful for fighting infections and supporting digestive health.

- **Nettle (Urtica dioica)**: Nettle is a nutritional powerhouse, rich in vitamins and minerals. It's excellent for detoxification, allergy relief, and supporting joint health.

- **Dandelion (Taraxacum officinale)**: Dandelion is a liver tonic, promoting detoxification and digestive health. Its leaves are nutrient-rich and can be used in salads or as a diuretic.

- **Mint (Mentha spp.)**: Mint is not only refreshing but also helps with digestion and can relieve symptoms of irritable bowel syndrome (IBS). Its cooling effect is also beneficial for relieving minor aches and pains.

- **Aloe Vera (Aloe barbadensis miller)**: Aloe Vera is a must for skin care, providing relief from burns, cuts, and other skin irritations. It can also be used internally for digestive health.

- **Cayenne (Capsicum annuum)**: Cayenne can boost metabolism, aid in digestion, and relieve pain when applied topically. It's also useful for stopping bleeding quickly.

- **Plantain Leaf (Plantago major)**: Plantain leaf is a natural remedy for cuts, insect bites, and skin irritations. Its astringent properties make it effective in wound healing and infection prevention.

- **Willow Bark (Salix spp.)**: Known as nature's aspirin, willow bark can relieve pain, inflammation, and fever. It's essential for natural pain management and reducing inflammation in the body.

Each of these herbs has been chosen for its versatility, effectiveness, and ease of use, making them foundational to any home apothecary. Whether you're dealing with minor health issues, looking to boost your immune system, or need ingredients for natural beauty products, these herbs cover a broad spectrum of uses that can address the needs of any household.

26.2: Seasonal Planting and Harvesting Tips

To ensure the highest quality and potency of your herbal remedies, timing your planting and harvesting according to the seasons is crucial. Here are detailed tips to guide you through the process:

Spring:

- **Start Seedlings Indoors**: Begin with seeds like basil, calendula, and chamomile indoors 6-8 weeks before the last frost. Use a well-draining soil mix in a sunny spot or under grow lights.

- **Prepare the Garden**: As the ground thaws, enrich your garden soil with compost to provide the nutrients your herbs will need. Ensure good drainage to prevent root rot.

- **Transplanting**: After the last frost, when the soil has warmed, transplant your seedlings outdoors. Acclimate them gradually to outdoor conditions over a week to prevent shock.

Summer:

- **Direct Sowing**: Herbs like dandelion, nettle, and mint can be directly sown into your garden as they thrive in warm soil. Plant in a location that receives at least six hours of sunlight daily.

- **Maintenance**: Keep the soil moist but not waterlogged. Mulch around the plants to retain moisture and suppress weeds. Regularly check for pests and diseases.

- **Harvesting**: Begin harvesting leaves as soon as the plant has enough foliage to maintain growth. Always harvest in the morning after the dew has evaporated but before the sun is too intense.

Autumn:

- **Late Planting**: Plant perennials like sage and rosemary now, as the cooler temperatures will allow them to establish roots without the stress of summer heat.

- **Harvesting Roots**: For herbs like ginger and turmeric, autumn is the time for harvesting roots. Wait until the foliage begins to die back, then gently dig around the plant to harvest.

- **Preparation for Winter**: Mulch your perennial herbs to protect them from freezing temperatures. Some herbs, like mint, can be invasive, so consider potting them to prevent spreading.

Winter:

- **Indoor Herbs**: Continue growing herbs like basil and chives indoors on a sunny windowsill or under grow lights to have fresh herbs year-round.

- **Planning**: Use this time to plan next year's garden. Research new herbs you'd like to try and order seeds in advance.

- **Rest and Maintenance**: Clean and sharpen your gardening tools, readying them for spring. Reflect on the past season's successes and challenges to improve your apothecary garden.

General Tips:

- **Watering**: Herbs generally prefer well-drained soil. Overwatering can lead to root diseases, so allow the soil to dry out slightly between watering.

- **Soil pH**: Most herbs thrive in a pH range of 6.0 to 7.0. Test your soil and amend it if necessary to meet these conditions.

- **Companion Planting**: Planting certain herbs together can benefit their growth and deter pests. For example, planting chives near roses can help repel aphids.

By following these seasonal planting and harvesting tips, you can maximize the health and potency of your herbal remedies. Each season brings its own set of tasks and rewards in the apothecary garden, offering a continuous cycle of growth, harvest, and renewal.

Chapter 27. Foraging Wild Herbs

27.1: Identifying Medicinal Plants Safely

When foraging for wild herbs, safety is paramount, not only to ensure that you're collecting the right plants but also to protect the ecosystem and yourself from harm. Here are detailed techniques and tools to help you identify medicinal plants safely:

Field Guides and Identification Apps: Arm yourself with a reputable field guide specific to the region you're foraging in. These guides often include high-quality photos and detailed descriptions of plants, including their habitat, leaf patterns, and flowering times. Identification apps can also be a valuable tool, offering the convenience of quick, in-field reference and often the ability to compare your photos with those in a database for a more accurate identification.

Take a Foraging Course: Participating in a local foraging course can provide hands-on experience with an expert who knows the local flora. This can dramatically improve your ability to identify plants safely and ethically. Courses often cover how to forage responsibly, preserving biodiversity and ensuring sustainability.

Use Sensory Checks: Many plants can be identified by their unique smell, texture, or even taste. However, taste testing should be done with extreme caution and only when you are nearly certain of a plant's identity, as some toxic plants can mimic edible ones closely. Crushing a leaf and smelling it, feeling the texture of the plant, and observing any milky sap or unique plant structures can all be clues to its identity.

Photograph and Document: When you find a plant you believe to be medicinal, take clear photographs of it, including close-ups of leaves, flowers, and any distinctive features. Document the location and the date of your find. This can help with later research and verification, especially if consulting with a more experienced forager or herbalist.

Carry the Right Tools: Equip yourself with a good quality magnifying glass to examine small plant details that might not be visible to the naked eye. A small trowel or shovel can be useful for gently uprooting plants, allowing you to examine the root structure, which is often a key identification feature. Always remember to fill any holes you make and disturb the site as little as possible.

Learn to Recognize Common Look-alikes: Many medicinal plants have non-medicinal or even toxic look-alikes. Familiarize yourself with these potential confusions to avoid dangerous mistakes. For example, the beneficial plantain (Plantago major) can be confused with the toxic lanceleaf plantain (Plantago lanceolata) by beginners.

Harvest Responsibly: Once you've positively identified a medicinal plant, ensure you harvest it responsibly. Take only what you need, leaving plenty for the plant to continue to grow, and for wildlife that might rely on it. Never uproot the entire plant unless it is abundant in the area and doing so won't harm the local ecosystem.

Consult with Local Herbalists and Foragers: Building a relationship with experienced foragers and herbalists in your area can be invaluable. They can offer insights into local plant life, share identification tips, and provide advice on sustainable foraging practices.

Practice Ethical Foraging: Always forage with respect for nature. Avoid foraging in protected areas or private property without permission. Be mindful of the impact your foraging has on the ecosystem, and strive to leave no trace of your presence.

By adhering to these techniques and utilizing the appropriate tools, you can safely identify and harvest medicinal plants from the wild. This not only enriches your apothecary with potent, natural remedies but also connects you deeply with the natural world, fostering a greater appreciation for the plants that grow in your region.

27.2: Ethical Foraging Practices

Ethical foraging practices are paramount to preserving the natural balance and ensuring that wild herbs continue to thrive for future generations. As you embark on your foraging journey, it's crucial to adopt a mindset of stewardship and respect towards nature. Here are specific guidelines to ensure your foraging activities are sustainable and ethical:

1. **Know the Local Regulations**: Before foraging, familiarize yourself with the local laws and regulations. Many areas have specific rules about what can be foraged and where. National parks, nature reserves, and private properties often have strict prohibitions or require permits. Abiding by these regulations protects natural habitats and respects the rights of landowners.

2. **Harvest Sustainably**: When you've identified a plant that's safe and legal to forage, use sustainable harvesting techniques to minimize your impact. For leafy herbs, take only one-third of the plant or less, allowing it to recover and continue growing. For roots, only harvest when there is an abundant population, and limit your collection to a small portion of the plants present.

3. **Avoid Rare or Endangered Species**: Educate yourself on the plants that are considered rare, threatened, or endangered in your area. These should never be foraged. Removing even a single specimen can have significant impacts on the survival of the species. Use reliable resources or consult with local experts to ensure you can identify and avoid these plants.

4. **Leave No Trace**: Practice the principle of "Leave No Trace" by not disturbing the surrounding area. Stick to established trails to avoid trampling undergrowth and compacting soil. If you dig up a plant, fill in the hole and replace the topsoil to protect the ecosystem.

5. **Use the Right Tools**: Employ the appropriate tools for foraging to ensure efficient and minimal impact harvesting. A sharp knife or scissors can cut plants cleanly without pulling up the roots. A small trowel is useful for digging, but make sure to disturb the soil as little as possible.

6. **Forage in Abundance**: Only forage in areas where the plant is abundant. Taking plants from a sparse population can hinder its ability to reproduce and thrive. This practice ensures that there will be plenty of herbs for wildlife, other foragers, and future growth.

7. **Spread Seed**: If you're harvesting seeds or fruits, consider spreading some as you go to encourage new growth. This helps to replenish what you've taken and supports the propagation of the plant species.

8. **Be Considerate of Wildlife**: Remember that you're sharing the space with wildlife that rely on these plants for food, shelter, and more. Be mindful of nesting sites and feeding areas, and avoid foraging in these sensitive spots.

9. **Clean and Inspect Your Harvest**: Before leaving the area, clean off any soil or debris to avoid transporting seeds of invasive species to new locations. Inspect your harvest for insects or diseases that could spread to your garden or home.

10. **Share Knowledge Respectfully**: If you're foraging with or teaching others, emphasize the importance of ethical practices. Encourage respect for nature and the sharing of knowledge in a way that promotes conservation and sustainability.

By adhering to these ethical foraging practices, you contribute to the health and longevity of wild herb populations and their ecosystems. This respectful approach ensures that these natural resources remain abundant and accessible for all who wish to connect with nature and harness the healing power of plants.

Chapter 28: Preservation Techniques

28.1: Drying, Freezing, and Infusing Herbs

Infusing Herbs offers a delightful way to preserve the essence and therapeutic properties of herbs. This method involves steeping herbs in a liquid to extract their flavors and medicinal qualities. The most common liquids used for infusions are **oil**, **alcohol**, and **vinegar**, each serving different purposes and shelf lives.

1. **Oil Infusions**: Ideal for creating massage oils, salves, and cooking ingredients. Choose a carrier oil like **olive oil**, **coconut oil**, or **sweet almond oil** for their stability and ability to extract the active compounds from herbs. Begin by filling a clean, dry jar about half to three-quarters full with dried herbs to prevent moisture from causing mold. Pour the carrier oil over the herbs until they are completely submerged, leaving about an inch of oil above the herbs to account for expansion. Seal the jar tightly and place it in a warm, sunny spot for 4 to 6 weeks, shaking it every few days to mix the contents. After the infusion period, strain the herbs from the oil using cheesecloth or a fine mesh strainer, squeezing out as much oil as possible. Store the infused oil in a cool, dark place. The shelf life can range from 1 to 2 years, depending on the oil used and storage conditions.

2. **Alcohol Infusions**: Alcohol is a powerful solvent that can extract a wide range of medicinal compounds, making it perfect for creating tinctures. Use a high-proof alcohol like **vodka** or **brandy**, which preserves the tincture and extracts the medicinal properties effectively. Fill a jar one-third to one-half with dried herbs, then pour in the alcohol, completely covering the herbs by at least two inches to allow for swelling. Seal the jar and store it in a cool, dark place, shaking it daily for 4 to 6 weeks. Strain the herbs using cheesecloth or a fine mesh strainer, and store the tincture in amber or blue dropper bottles to protect it from light. Alcohol tinctures can last for several years when stored properly.

3. **Vinegar Infusions**: Vinegar infusions are excellent for culinary uses and some health applications, such as digestive tonics. Apple cider vinegar is preferred for its health benefits and pleasant taste. Fill a jar with dried herbs to about one-third full, then cover with apple cider vinegar, ensuring the herbs are completely submerged to prevent mold. Seal the jar with a plastic lid or place parchment paper under a metal lid to prevent corrosion from the vinegar. Store the jar in a cool, dark place, shaking it daily for 2 to 4 weeks. Strain the herbs and transfer the vinegar to clean bottles. Vinegar infusions can last up to a year when stored in a cool, dark place.

Labeling is crucial for all infusions, including the date of creation and ingredients. Always use **dried herbs** to minimize water content, which can lead to spoilage. Each method of infusing herbs offers a unique way to capture and preserve their healing properties, enhancing your culinary dishes, health routines, and natural medicine cabinet.

Conclusion: The Importance of Herbalism

Embracing the ancient art of herbalism is not merely a return to traditional healing methods; it is a profound journey towards self-sufficiency and wellness in our modern world. The knowledge and skills you have acquired through this guide empower you to harness the natural world's vast healing potential, offering a sustainable alternative to conventional medicine. By integrating these ancient remedies and herbal formulas into your daily life, you are taking a significant step towards enhancing your health, resilience, and independence.

The practice of creating your own apothecary is a deeply rewarding experience that connects you with the rhythms of nature and the wisdom of our ancestors. It encourages a holistic approach to health, where prevention and natural balance are prioritized over the reactive treatment of symptoms. This shift in perspective is not only beneficial for your physical well-being but also for your mental and emotional health. As you cultivate, harvest, and prepare your remedies, you develop a closer relationship with the plants that support your health, deepening your understanding of their properties and the ways they can be used to heal and nourish your body.

Moreover, building your survival apothecary equips you with the tools and knowledge necessary to face a wide range of health challenges and emergencies. Whether it's crafting a simple herbal tea to soothe a sore throat or preparing a comprehensive kit for natural first aid, the skills you've learned are invaluable assets in both everyday life and unexpected situations. This self-reliance not only enhances your personal resilience but also allows you to support and care for your community in times of need.

As you continue to explore the world of herbalism, remember that this journey is one of constant learning and discovery. The landscape of natural healing is vast, with countless plants and remedies still waiting to be explored. Each step you take deepens your connection with the natural world, enriching your life with the wisdom and healing power of plants.

To truly embrace the art of herbalism, it's essential to approach it with both curiosity and a willingness to experiment. Your apothecary, whether it's a small shelf in your kitchen or a dedicated room in your home, is a testament to the power of nature and your ability to co-create with it. This space becomes a sanctuary where you can retreat to blend, brew, and concoct remedies that not only heal but also comfort and rejuvenate. It's a place where science meets intuition, and where each herb, with its unique properties, contributes to the symphony of natural healing.

Engaging in the practice of herbalism also invites you to become part of a community of like-minded individuals who share your passion for natural wellness. Through workshops, online forums, and local gatherings, you can exchange knowledge, experiences, and discoveries, further enriching your understanding and appreciation of herbal medicine. This sense of community not only supports your own journey but also helps to revive and spread the ancient wisdom of herbal healing, making it accessible to more people.

As you integrate herbal remedies into your life, you'll find that many of the plants you work with are not only healers but also teachers. They offer lessons in patience, care, and the interconnectedness of all living things. This deepens your respect for the environment and inspires a commitment to sustainability and conservation, ensuring that these healing plants will continue to thrive for generations to come.

Incorporating herbal practices into your daily routine can be as simple as starting your day with a cup of herbal tea that energizes or soothes, depending on your needs. It could also mean reaching for a homemade salve or tincture when you or a family member needs relief from minor ailments. These small acts of self-care are powerful affirmations of your ability to nurture and heal, reinforcing the value of natural remedies in maintaining wellness.

Remember, the path of herbalism is one of exploration and personal growth. It encourages you to listen to your body and to nature, to observe, learn, and adapt. There's no end to the knowledge you can acquire; each plant, each remedy, brings with it a story, a history, and a wealth of healing potential. By choosing this path, you're not just preparing for emergencies or seeking alternatives to conventional medicine; you're also embracing a way of life that celebrates the beauty and abundance of the natural world.

Your journey into herbalism is a powerful statement of independence, resilience, and a deep-seated belief in the healing power of nature. It's a commitment to a healthier, more sustainable way of living that honors the wisdom of the past while looking forward to a future where natural healing is revered and practiced widely. As you continue to walk this path, let your curiosity guide you, let your discoveries inspire you, and let the healing power of plants transform you and those around you.

Made in the USA
Middletown, DE
27 April 2025

74802572R00097